HOW TO IMPROVE WORK BEHAVIOR

BY

M. KUKREJA, M.D.

HOW TO IMPROVE WORK BEHAVIOR

"S.O. R.E.A.C.T."

BY
M. KUKREJA M.D.

COPYRIGHT © 2020

ISBN# 978-0-578-69187-9

Please note that the word "he" is used for convenience in this book. Everything applies to men and women as far as possible.

THIS BOOK IS DEDICATED
TO PEOPLE EVERYWHERE.

THINGS TO REMEMBER

How can you survive if you do not value yourself, your work, health, money, and time?

Your work is as important as your family or personal life, not more, not less.

If you lie and manipulate, you will lose your credibility both at work and in your family.

Do not waste your life repeating the mistakes of others. Learn from their experiences.

Protect the reputation of your colleagues.

Protect your dignity as well as the dignity of the other person.

Do not burn your bridges when you leave your job. You never know when your path may again cross that of your employer. Be professional and offer excellence until the end.

Five minutes before leaving for work, you should sit down and become completely calm.

S.O. R.E.A.C.T.

SPEECH

ORGANIZE

RELATIONSHIPS

EXCELLENCE

APPEARANCE

CHARACTER

TIME

Contents

PREFACE

It is significant whether one values oneself and equally vital, how much one values work and money!

If work is smooth sailing for you, you can put this book down. It is not for you. It is written with others in mind. If, however, you are just entering the workforce and are looking to improve your work experience or wanting to become a better employee or an employer, keep reading.

It is not enough to finish high school or university and go off to work. After all, you do not go to war without your weapons! You must polish certain qualities in your behavior first, whether you are a clerk or a doctor. Add cheerfulness and tact. They are the icing on the cake!

This book is designed as a resource for people entering the workforce, those who are already working but who wish to improve their performance, and those who want their children to have an advantage in the workforce. It is necessary to teach proper "work behavior" to your children or students if you want them to be productive and society to prosper. Work behavior must be taught from middle school.

We behave according to our habits or our character without thinking. But it is very important to consciously plan every morning how we are going to behave that day. Are we going to be irritable or calm, rude or courteous, arrogant or helpful? We cannot do this unless we are strong and have self-control.

This book is also written for those who have problems at work that they do not know how to resolve.

They may be highly intelligent but are quite unhappy at the workplace. They may have experienced friction at work, received warnings, lost their jobs repeatedly, and do not know why. They wonder what it is that others have that they do not. Such persons may blame their employers and keep making the same mistakes.

It is designed for those who wish to be better employers. Whether you want to earn a paycheck or start a business, the foundation is the same. You must be a good employee in order to be a good boss.

The book has also tried to reach out to those who are" outliers" to the so-called social norms.

It has addressed the effect of abuse in one's personal life on one's work performance.

It is not enough to have work skills. *It is also who one is, as a person, which is equally important.* You see people behaving with curiosity or fear, self-confidence or an inferiority complex, rudeness or diplomacy, and cheerfulness or depression. There is a difference between working with an angry person or one who is relaxed. All these affect our work behavior and success.

Some people learn the right work behavior from their families and prosper. Some come from families that do not know, and so cannot impart, the proper behavior. These people are left behind or ruined on the road of life. They have nowhere to turn and no one to teach them. This book is one of the places they may turn to.

The author has introduced an acronym, R.E.A.C.T., which should help the reader remember the qualities needed for working.

Some of the rules may not be applicable in the present times of epidemic because you are working from home. However, the qualities remain consistent.

How sad it is to be afraid of working. It is the unknown of which we are most fearful. We need clarity of vision.

It is a shame to waste your potential! It is very wrong to want to live on your savings when you are capable of working. Even if you are rich, your goal should be to double your money, not finish it for pleasure. It is sad not to value work. Work makes life meaningful.

As a physician, one sees repetitively the employer and the employed, as well as the abused and the abuser. The doctor sees the stress from work and the medical complications from this. Some of these could have been avoided had one known the correct path.

They say that when one is ready to learn, a teacher appears. I hope that this book brings you some clarity on questions you may have.

M. Kukreja, M.D.

FOREWORD

I enjoyed reading "How to Improve Work Behavior" by Dr. Kukreja and I thought this was a highly organized manual for anyone who wants to be a better employee (or a better employer), for anyone who is first starting on a career, and generally, anyone seeking to better their day-to-day work experience.

I liked the way the book is divided into ten parts covering a wide spectrum of employment and its varied situations, motivations, difficulties, influences of family background, and numerous other factors, all of which give the reader a broad understanding of the employment world.

In my opinion, this is a practical book to read once and then have on hand for future reference and guidance.

Finally, I liked the way the book was concluded in Part Ten on how to raise children to help them get ready for the workplace.

Very well done, and I highly recommend this book.

Don Sebastian and TeamGolfWell.

PART ONE: WORK BASICS

CHAPTER 1: BASIC WORK HABITS

Whether you are a child living at home, a student in a dorm, a housewife, self-employed, or work for someone, certain work habits are essential to acquire if you want peace of mind and not waste your time.

Put similar things in the same place.

Store the same items together. For example, do not put one bar of soap on one side of the room or a cabinet and the second bar on the other side.

Designate an area

An example is putting all the things you need to take home together in a designated corner.

Scan the area you are entering.

Look to see if there is anything unusual in the grounds, room, or car before you enter.

When you leave a place, room, or vehicle, always look back to see that you did not forget anything.

Did you leave your purse, file, or coat? Do you have to go back and pick up something else that you forgot?

Do your work in the same order to avoid forgetting something.

For example, when turning your car off, do it in the same order. First, close the windows, then turn off your lights, and then turn off your ignition. Or always pick up your phone and keys before you leave a place.

Take care of a thing then and there as far as possible. or write it down.

If something has fallen, put it in its right place immediately. If the toilet tissue roll is finished, replace it before doing anything else. Do not put off a thing for later unless it will take more than two minutes and you are engrossed in something urgent. In such a case, write yourself a reminder to do it once you have finished your work.

Give yourself an obvious reminder.

When you must remember to do something, e.g., pick up your laundry, put an object out of its place in the room to remind you.

Be Neat.

Your brain utilizes less energy to accomplish things when it works in a neat and organized place. Neatness teaches you how to organize and brings self-discipline, qualities needed for life. You do not waste precious time looking for things. Therefore, you do not get nervous, anxious or frustrated.

Work in a clean and neat environment, not a dirty or a messy one.

Before you start your day, see that your bed is made, your room is neat, and that you are clean and neat.

Prepare before you start your work.

Take out all the tools you need and see that they are in working order before you start a project

See that you have enough supplies of everything needed before starting your project.

Finish a station before you start your next station.

Finish what you began before starting something else, or else put it in a neat separate pile or write it down. Suppose you were interrupted to bring something into a room. Put it away, or into a corner, before resuming your work.

When you finish a project, put away all things and papers connected with it before starting your next project.

If you cannot do so because of a priority, keep all items connected to it in a separate saved area.

After the age of two, a child should not have more than two toys scattered outside. He can be shown to put away his other toys before playing with these two. Also, before he goes to bed, he should put all his toys in a box or basket in the room. This way, he gets used to neat surroundings.

However, do not enforce this if the child is sick or tired.

A structured way of doing things must always be accompanied by flexibility.

Have a list.

Make a list of what you need to do the following day.

Always prioritize your list.

If there is no priority, try to do the phone calls first. Also, do the things that will take the least time first to get them out of the way.

Prepare for things ahead.

Check your things the day before to see that you have everything. This includes school bags, notebooks, pens, keys, IDs, money, clothes for the next day etc.

Prepare for any meeting that you are going to. What information are you looking for? What questions will you be asked? Do you have all your receipts and invoices? Do you have the dates of your prior appointments associated with this? This also applies if you are meeting a repairer.

Have a folder for items that you are waiting for a response.

Have a fixed day when you pay your bills, or do you pay them as they come in?

Fix a day monthly to have a financial meeting with yourself.

That is the day to go over your financial situation and check your outstanding balances or bills with questions.

Be clear about your duties.

When you take a new job, ask and be very clear about what is expected from you and your work duties.

Settle down first.

When you arrive at your work, put away your things, keys, and purse, and settle down before you start working.

Work fast. Work hard.

Do not be lazy. What counts is "how much work you put in the time, not how much time you put in the work."

Offer excellence in your work.

Take a break.

Like physical work, intense mental activity needs you to take some time off to refresh yourself and charge your battery.

Prepare before you leave.

See that your workplace is clean and neat after you finish and before you leave.

Check your list of things to do before you leave a room or a place. This includes seeing that all the lights and machines are shut off and that you have your keys.

Before you retire or go to sleep, see that you are prepared for the next day. Put things back in their place. Empty your purse of any unnecessary items. Check that you have your keys, money and phone. This way, you do not waste time looking for them the next day.

Use your calendar.

Mark the date on your calendar as to when you should be checking on a project.

6

Write important events, appointments, and follow-up dates on your calendar. Staple the appointments cards on the corresponding month in your calendar.

Arrive 15 minutes before any appointment. Give yourself time for delay as in missing a bus. Check the route the day before if necessary

Shopping

Read the papers and check the money given to you before leaving a counter.

Make a list before you go shopping so that you do not waste your time.

Decide how much you are willing to spend before you go shopping.

Look at the supplies given to you before you leave the place. Make sure that you have gotten everything you asked for.

Never be on your cell phone while you are dealing with a cashier. It shows that you are addicted to your phone and lack good manners.

Get a thing while you still have one item of it (for example, sugar). Do not wait until you run out of it.

Do not hoard.

Get rid of anything that you have not used for two years.

Have a routine

in the morning, after you wake up,

After you reach work,

before you leave work,

after you come home,

and in the evening before you go to bed.

Sleep

Wake up and sleep at the same time every day.

Close all stimulatory devices, such as iPads or iPhones, one hour before sleeping.

CHAPTER 2: THE TONE OF YOUR VOICE

How you speak is critical to your success.

In speaking, you must protect your dignity, and you must protect the dignity of the other person.

The tone of your voice.

You should have one of the following tones:

a cheerful tone,

a respectful tone.

an even tone,

a non-committal tone,

a calm tone or

a friendly tone.

What you should not have, is an accusatory, angry, non-caring, insulting, or contemptuous tone.

It is when something unexpected happens that your true tone comes out. How do you react? Suppose your child carelessly lost the key, and now you are locked out. Do you develop an angry, accusatory tone? Do you attack and say, "I told you to check the key before we left!" Or can you still have an even tone and say, "Hmm, we are locked out. Let me see what I can do about this?"

How Do You Speak?

The "Do's"

Listen more than you speak.

Be courteous.

Be cheerful.

Be caring.

Make people feel comfortable.

Talk in a relaxed manner.

Be helpful and hopeful.

Let the other person finish talking before you jump in.

Do not interrupt him or her.

See the time and place before you speak.

See if this is the right time to speak.

See if the person is too overwhelmed or emotional to understand what you say.

See if the other person will be able to understand what you say?

> Do not teach rocket science to a child. Do not teach pregnancy to a child.

See if the other person will be receptive to what you say. Do not tell things to someone who does not respect you, who considers you wrong or stupid, who has made up his mind that he does not like you or feels that you are depriving him of his power.

Sometimes you have to throw a seed into the soil and hope it takes root.

Do not give advice more than once.

Let the other person "save face."

That means letting him have a way out without losing his self-respect.

Defuse the situation.

Bring people together.

The "Do Nots"

Do not talk fast.

No one can understand you. The purpose of language is to be understood. This is critical when you are dealing with a customer over the phone.

There should be no disrespect.

Do not talk to those, senior to you, in position or age, as if they are your equal.

Never say, "I was talking first."

If the other person interrupts or speaks at the same time, stop and say, "Please go ahead." Let him speak first. It is a sign of good manners. Hear him completely. Your company's welfare depends on this.

Do not sound impatient or disdainful.

It is the easiest way to lose a customer or a friend.

Do not refuse to help.

"I already gave you this information." If he asks, you should give the information again.

Do not be condescending

Do not act as if you are talking to a child. If you were told to understand plumbing at the first shot, you could not.

Do not keep repeating a statement.

"Sir, the company policy is and so on". He heard you the first time.

Do not use your tongue as a weapon to attack others,

Do not insult, humiliate, demean, or make fun of them. There is to be no contempt in your words or attitude.

Do not shout at others.

Do not talk in a scolding or intimidating way.

Do not speak as if you are cross-examining unless you are really cross-examining ("Did you do this? Did you put the correct stamps? Did you take your medicine?"). Say People should feel comfortable around you.

Never take a person's self-confidence away by the way you talk.

Do not embarrass a person in front of his family.

This includes questioning his professional knowledge.

There should be no counterattacking.

An example is when someone reproaches or advises you. Instead of listening, you counter-attack because you do not like to be on the defensive.

General rules

Do not be a hypocrite. Do not talk nicely to someone at his face but gossip about him behind his back.

Do not ruin anyone's reputation.

Do not divide people. Do not turn one against another.

Do not join in the criticism of another. Never have a mob mentality.

Try not to scold in front of others.

Wait until you calm down. Do not scold him then and there.

CHAPTER 3: CONGRATULATIONS!

Congratulations! You have got a job! All those study hours and examinations have paid off. You now have a degree. You are ready to enter the job market.

But let me tell you a secret. It is not enough!

It is not enough to be willing to work. It is not enough to have the knowledge and technical skills. You have the skills for the trade. After all, you have a degree. But it is still not enough. Companies are now acknowledging what has been known for a long time to employers:

You need other skills besides your degrees or a willingness to learn.

Some companies refer to them as "soft skills," but there is nothing "soft" about them. They are so critical that you will get fired if you do not have them, despite being a worker and despite your degree.

These boil down to your work behavior.

Employers can see your education and experience in your CV or resume, but they cannot tell anything about your "work behavior" until they see you working. Therefore, the employer needs a trial period, which may range from one day to three months. Certain work conditions may make you flourish while others do not, and this is not a reflection on you. First, however, the employer has to see whether you will fit into his environment.

Yes, you need knowledge and skills. Yes, performance improves with experience. But values and behavior are just as important in work culture. Nothing hurts you so much in work as arrogance, carelessness, anger, and lacking the following: self-value, the value of work, self-confidence, focus, and inter-personal skills. Is it not great that you possess these already?

When you are not doing well at work, check to see what is lacking. Do you fit into the office culture? Do you consider office events important? Have you the discipline to finish your work in time? Can you handle criticism? Can you get along with others? Do you feel that you know how to do your business and your employer should not tell you what to do or how to do it? Do you ignore instructions? Do you make your own decisions at the workplace without checking what the policy is? Are you distracted by family issues or by a relationship? Do you have contempt for others? Can you control your temper?

> Know that if you rebel against authority at home, you will rebel against authority at work and thus will not be successful.

You do not belong in the workplace if you are rebelling against authority, if you are busy insisting that you are just as important as the next person, if you feel that you know more than your boss, if you are a bully, and if you do not know how to treat people with respect. The next chapter goes into further details.

Sometimes you may have a job that you hate, or you may think that you have a calling to be an artist or a writer. You still must keep the job that you have until you can find another one, or your calling can feed you. You must sustain yourself and always put food on the table.

CHAPTER 4: WHY WOULD YOU STILL FAIL?

Why would you still fail despite your skills?

If you keep yourself occupied on the social media with only mindless chatter, dancing, fashion and music, you will be left behind in the job market.

This is because you do not know of events happening around you or in the world. You do not know anything about the sciences, the arts, the present social upheavals or past history, political and otherwise, of the world.

You may not care that you are ignorant. But employers and companies do. They will not want to present an employee to their clients and customers if he cannot hold an intelligent conversation about events having nothing to do with the company.

Having knowledge only helps you to grow and prevents others from having pity on you.

Other factors causing you to fail

How you speak,

No self-value,

No self-confidence,

No self-discipline,

No value of work, money, or time,

Addiction,

Laziness,

Distracted over what is happening in your personal
life,

No control over emotions,

No clarity of how to behave at work,

No motivation,

No enthusiasm,

Your home is a battlefront

You value your home over your work and

Luck.

CHAPTER 5: WHY SHOULD YOU VALUE WORK?

1. Work gives you money.

Money helps you survive by giving you the ability to get the necessities of life.

Money gives you the freedom to buy some of the things that you want and even luxuries.

It protects you from the abuse and contempt of others.

Money gives you power.

It helps you to gain independence in planning and making decisions.

It can pay for your education or that of others.

It gives you the ability to help others and give to charity.

But do not be so arrogant as to think that since with your money, you support others, including your spouse and children, therefore, you should have absolute power! Rest assured that if you drop dead tomorrow, they will still be fed and be taken care of.

A man who has inherited a large sum of money should work to double it, not waste it. You are not supposed to live off your inheritance or savings when you are in the prime of your health. You must show that you can support yourself.

2. But work brings other benefits.

Work brings you self-respect and self-confidence as you support yourself and your family.

Work enables you to show others what you are capable of.

It gives you self-discipline.

It shows you the need to focus, be organized, and work fast.

3. Work gives you knowledge.

Work enables you to learn skills.

It enables you to meet others, exchange ideas, and learn from them on different topics.

4. Work can change your life.

You may have the opportunity to travel because of your work.

You may move to a different job or position.

You may meet people who may lead you to a different path.

5. Work gives you social support and friendships.

You meet people and make friends at work.

You can develop social support that will help you in your time of need.

When you value work, you will act professionally.

One of the ways of being professional is the ability to prevent your personal life from affecting your *behavior* at work. You cannot be pleasant at one time and rude at another and excuse yourself by saying that you have had a bad day or that a lot is happening in your personal life. You should have the same even attitude regardless.

> You cannot allow your personal life to affect your performance at work.

Work hard. Work so that your employers will want to hire you again. Work hard until the last day, even after you have handed in your resignation. That is acting professionally. Even if you are leaving your place of employment, you will need that reference in the future.

Keep quiet even if you do not think that the work is being handled in the best way. Do not try to change the workplace. It is easier for your boss to remove you instead.

CHAPTER 6: THE SEVEN STEPS

There are seven critical steps in work when you are dealing with customers:

1. How you look to a customer.

   (Relaxed, attentive, harried, nervous, irritable, angry, or arrogant).

2. How you approach a customer.

   (Friendly, courteous, rude, arrogant, impatient, or helpful).

3. How you speak to a customer.

   (Courteous, considerate, patient, or rude and argumentative. Never imply to a patient that he is stupid because he does not understand you).

4. How you perform your work.

   (Excellent or slipshod. Do you cheat? Do you waste your time?)

5. How you follow up or standby your work.

   (Are you willing to replace a defective material and absorb the cost? Are you willing to go beyond your duty and help the customer?)

6. Are you dependable?

7. Do you value time?

CHAPTER 7: WHY WOULD YOUR EMPLOYER KEEP YOU?

Do you like your work and your workplace? Are you happy to get up from your bed every morning and head off to work? Are you learning things at your workplace? Are you contributing to the smooth running of your company? Your company is fortunate to have you.

But perhaps things could be a little better if only you knew what exactly was wrong. Right now, you are getting through work, equipped only with the knowledge of how you saw your parents perform and how the actors on the television show you how to work. You have the knowledge and the skills required.

If only there were a checklist that you could glance through.

That list is presented in various forms in this book. It is wonderful that you can go through the list with flying colors. There are only a few things that need tweaking, and you are on your way. But the "things" are different for everyone, so the list, and the book containing it, are presented in their entirety. Knowledge is power, and anything is better than stumbling in the dark.

One should start with the question of why any employer will keep any employee.

Your goal should be to help your employer run his company smoothly *in the manner that he wants.*

It is great that you have good skills. But it is equally critical to get along with your employer, seniors, colleagues, juniors, and your customers.

If you cannot focus, if you cannot follow your employer's instructions, if you are disrespectful and cannot handle criticism, you are not helping your employer. Why then would your employer keep you? It may not be easy, but truthful self-reflection and assessment are necessary if you want to improve your work behavior.

Why would your boss give you a paycheck if you do the following ten things?

1. You are not pleasant to be around, even with your boss.

No one wants to keep an angry or rude personality, no matter how good he is as a worker.

<u>Your attitude is:</u>

You become aggressive or argumentative with people who disagree with you or correct you.

You think you have a right to be rude to others as long as you do your work well.

You believe that your rights supersede the necessity to be cordial to others.

2. You cannot focus and work in a distracted manner. You do things right half the time.

<u>Your attitude is:</u>

You feel that at the times when you do things wrongly, it is not important since you do them well at other times.

3. You do not offer excellence.

4. You refuse to follow the instructions of your employer.

<u>Your attitude is:</u>

You feel that he has no business telling you to do anything since you have enough experience to do it in a different way.

You tell him that you know a better way to do things than he does.

You feel that your previous employers knew how to do things better than him.

5. You do not protect the office. Critical things are not put away. Important messages are not delivered to your employer immediately. Things that need immediate repairs or attention are not communicated. If help is needed at the workplace, you refuse to go.

<u>Your attitude is:</u>

You feel these responsibilities are not your problem.

6. You have no respect for your employer. You have contempt for him. You damage his reputation.

<u>Your attitude is:</u>

You want to show him that he cannot mess around with you.

7. You do not value time. You are late or leave early. You do not finish projects by the deadline. You take excessive time off.

<u>Your attitude is:</u>

You think that you work well when you are at work, so punctuality and presence should not matter.

You assume that your employer needs you, so he will put up with it.

8. You are not conscientious.

9. You are dishonest.

10. You cannot handle criticism constructively.

You take it as a personal attack and fight back or go around with an angry or sorrowful face. It does not occur to you to not take criticism personally but to see it as a chance to change your behavior. You cannot apologize and agree to do it differently.

Your attitude is:
You respond with, "How dare he talk to me like that? I am going to quit."

Would you keep someone if he behaved like this to you?

This is in stark contrast to one who is honest, respectful, follows instructions, focuses on his work, offers excellence, and is pleasant to be with. Why is it so difficult to be like this?

Understand that if there is friction more than twice between you and your boss, your days are numbered at the workplace.

CHAPTER 8: EMPLOYEE-EMPLOYER RELATIONSHIP

The way you feel about your employer is *always* picked up by him, no matter how much you may try to hide it. If you feel contempt for him, it will show in your eyes, or he will sense it!

> Your looks, posture, and demeanor can convey feelings of superiority over your employer

If you make fun of him behind his back, rest assured that word will get back to him. Someone will try to gain favor by informing him of what you are saying. Why then would he keep you? Are you not sabotaging your career?

You may think that the people to whom you are criticizing your boss are sympathizing with you. What do you expect them to say? They will be non-committal. They will hear you out. They may appear to agree with you. They will not waste their time fighting with you over this. But they value their career too much to join you. They may see your show of superiority as a lack of interpersonal skills and self-destructiveness. So, you will become an outsider. Does this make you a happy person?

Why would you want to treat your employer with contempt? Why would you want him to run the company the way you think is desirable? Why would you not care to correct the mistakes he points out to you? Why would you fight with him? Why would you want to show him that he cannot mess with you?

Why would you treat your colleagues in the workplace with contempt? Why would you speak disparagingly about them behind their backs? Why would you make them look bad?

Perhaps you are doing this unconsciously. Do not repeat the same mistake. Unfortunately, some people spend their whole life doing this. Think about how this will affect your life. The consequences can be dire. The word will get around about you. Your employer will not give good references for you. In the end, you may never be given work again in your life. Do you really want to stay at home, bored out of your mind?

Think about this.

Would you want to hire someone to work for you if you knew that he felt superior to you? Would you keep such a person once you found out? Why behave like this yourself? Are you not being self-destructive? Do you know of anyone who would like to stay with a person who treats him with contempt unless he is helpless and abused?

Your reasons are not known even to you

Usually, this is unconscious behavior. When we do not know how we are behaving, and how this is hurting us, it is called a lack of insight.

1. You are arrogant. You think you know more than others. People who are arrogant do not think about the consequences of their behavior.

2. You have an inferiority complex.

People with an inferiority complex can only feel superior by making others feel inferior.

3. You may be unconsciously imitating your parent! This is how your parent behaved. Perhaps there was a struggle for power between your parents. The one who had the power held the others in contempt, and now you want to be powerful. Or maybe you come from a home where there was abuse, and now you would rather be the abuser than abused.

4. You come from a wealthy family. You do not really need the money.

5. You were spoiled and not taught to respect those who are seniors to you.

6. You were not taught interpersonal skills.

7. You were not taught how to respond to criticism.

8. You were not taught to value hierarchy.

9. You rebel against any authority. In a household of abuse, there is a rebellion against authority by the one who is grabbing power. That is what you have learned. There is only one consequence of rebelling against authority. You are thrown out, whether it is from the family, school, or employment.

10. You have no gratitude for having employment.

The minute you feel that you have been wronged, your instinct is to show them not to mess with you. You will put them in their place. You will show them that they are wrong, and you are right. You forget the big picture here. You have come to work and earn a reputation for being a good worker, quiet and dignified.

What is the advantage of treating your boss with respect and cooperation?

What is the advantage of showing respect, following orders, and not repeating your mistakes? Well, there will be minimal, if any, friction. When you value your work, you do not repeat your mistakes. You have the satisfaction of doing a job well. Meantime, trust is formed between your employer and you. He, in turn, begins to respect not only your talent but also your integrity. You will continue to learn and have a solid career. Why would he want to remove you? Even if you decide to leave, you will get a good reference. They will be happy to hire you again. So, who is being benefitted here? You are!

Your opinion

When your boss asks for everyone's opinion before deciding, note the following:

First, he is not looking for others to be a mere "yes." But the "no" has to be said tactfully.

Second, the closer you are to your boss, the more important it is that you give your suggestion to him privately so that others in the group do not feel that you are leading your boss.

Once you gave him your opinion, give him the time and space to reflect upon it without your presence.

Then accept whatever decision he finally makes and follow it even if you do not agree with it. Do not argue with him. You have chosen him as your leader.

Your goal is to help your leader to lead his vision smoothly. You are a part of a group, and the goals of the group are more important than your personal feelings unless they violate your moral ethics.

Scenarios of negative employee-employer relationships.

You have joined a company similar to your prior one. You believe that your old company ran the office differently, and in your opinion, in a much better way. You do not feel that your current employer is capable of taking the company anywhere. You state this to anyone who will listen.

Your previous and present companies are similar. Since you had twenty years of experience in the previous company, you feel that you know what changes to implement better than your employer, who is fairly young. But he will not listen to you. So, you complain to everyone.

You worked in a large company where you, as the administrative secretary, handled many subdivisions. Now you are in a small office with only one or two employees. Your attitude shows that you feel this is far beneath you.

You work in a company similar to your prior one. But the business is slow here, whereas your previous company was always busy. Your contempt for this company shows.

CHAPTER 9: WORK AND WOMAN

A woman needs the same skills, interpersonal relationships, and dedication as a man at the workplace. She, too, has to offer excellence and value time, but a woman must face other problems as well.

1. She is sexually harassed and

2. Her boss tries to have an affair with her. She makes the mistake of falling in love with her manager

3. She ignores warnings from her well-wishers.

These three things will ruin her life.

We will start with the warnings first.

Warnings.

When she is warned by her colleagues or friends about a man, she promptly informs the man and turns against the advisors.

Thus, she puts herself further in the power of the man in question.

A warning is just that, a warning for your welfare. How you deal with it will decide whether you will make a mistake and ruin your life

If someone warns you about your boss's personality, do not inform him and assure him that you do not believe this.

Nothing could be more stupid than this. The person warning you is trying to save you from heartache. So, keep silent about your warning. Have the intelligence to be forewarned and be on your guard.

Do not think that your honesty and true love should reveal this to the person concerned. Do not do so if you value yourself. If you value yourself, you protect yourself. Do not let him know what you have heard but be on your guard and do not put yourself in any compromising situations.

Harassment.

A girl working in an office faces different scenarios than a boy

1. You may be subject to sexual jokes, pictures, or innuendos.
2. You may be subjected to unwanted touching, a pat, or brushing by, leaning forward suddenly so that his arm goes past your chest or a hand that stays too long on your body

This is sexual harassment.

Say, "I do not like this." If he touches you, say, "Please do not do that," and move away. Move away if he comes too close. If he asks, "are you afraid of me?" say, "I am not comfortable. I would like to keep my distance."

Do not ignore it. Do not be quiet about it. If he threatens your job, record him. Report this to his boss and to the "Human Resources" in his company immediately

3. Your boss may try to have an affair with you.

4. You may be asked to work late alone with your manager.

Say your family will not approve. Ask if another person can work with you.

In the worst scenario, check your exits. Be on your guard. Check if you have a defensive item, even a knife. Have someone call you every half an hour. Have someone come to the office to pick you up or just wait outside the office room.

Note: Anyone who is an honorable person would not ask you to work with him alone in his office after hours.

5. Refuse if he asks you to dinner with him.

Say that your family or friends are waiting for you and that you cannot disappoint them. Then add, "I am not comfortable having dinner alone with my employer."

Your professional life and your personal life must be kept separate.

Now, he may turn around and accuse you of attacking his character. But he would never do so if he has a good character. This is manipulation. Just say, "Sorry, sir."

6. Refuse if you are offered to be dropped home by your employer

If your boss thinks that you are at risk by going home alone, he should send you home in a taxi or company car. But if he says that he is going in the direction of your home and can drop you, you should refuse.

7. He wants to pick up a file in his apartment and wants you to come along or see you when you are alone in your apartment.

Do not go to his apartment alone or invite him to your apartment. *This is not broadmindedness.* Does a chicken stay alone with a lion? The chicken wants to protect itself. What about you? You are giving permission to be raped.

8. He wants to find out if you are vulnerable.

Do not discuss anything about your family or your past with your boss. Stick to the barest minimum. Do not talk about your dreams, your losses, or your sorrows. Do not tell him if you live alone. He has no business trying to find these details unless his intentions are dishonorable. Change the subject, or ask, "Will there be anything else, sir?"

9. He wants to make you feel sorry for him

He tells you how lonely he is at home and how unhappy. Listen quietly without comment while looking down. Have no eye contact.

Note: It is not professional for a boss to have an affair with his employee.

Why does your boss behave thus?

a. He thinks that he is in a position of power and therefore is "entitled to some privileges."

b. He sees you as a conquest.

c. The most common reason is that he feels old and just wants to have a fling to prove that he is still attractive.

The more inferiority complex he has, the more he will want to prove this to himself.

d. Because he is not honorable, he is looking to have his cake and eat it too. He wants all the conveniences of his married life. He does not want the entanglement and expense of a divorce, but he also wants the thrill of an affair. But of course, he cannot tell you that. So, he needs a strategy.

The fact that he keeps it secretive shows that he knows that it is wrong.

Tactics applied to you

Your manager took a long time to reach his current position. That means he is older and now is ahead of you in manipulation.

1. He has to show you that he finds you attractive.

He may start giving you the long silent looks. Then come the compliments.

2. He has to make you feel sorry for him.

He will hint that he is misunderstood at home, or is not happy in his marriage, or despite his marriage, is lonely.

Note: If he is unhappy, no one is stopping him from leaving his family.

3. He will attribute magical powers to your personality.

"You make me feel alive and young. You are so intelligent. You approach things differently."

Note: It is not your job to make anyone feel alive. It is your body that makes him feel young.

4. <u>He has to lie to you.</u>

"I did not tell you before that I was married because I did not want to lose you."

Note: any action that is based on a lie is made by a dishonorable person.

He will say, "It just happened. I could not help falling in love with you."

Note: He is studying you to see how far he can manipulate you. Ask your father.

5. <u>He will string you along.</u>

"I am eventually going to get a divorce. This is not the right time. It will hurt my children.

Note: He thinks that you are not very intelligent and will fall for this line.

If he really wanted you, he would divorce his wife and marry you. But until then, he will not go to bed with you. He would not keep his affair quiet. He is keeping it quiet because he knows that people will say that his actions are wrong.

He also does not think that you have much self-respect and are willing to be a "kept woman." he can put you up in an apartment and still enjoy his married life. He really does not have a good opinion of you at all.

Are these tactics new? No. they are centuries old!

Your reactions

Let us get one thing straight. You were not going to the office to marry your boss or anyone superior. You do not want to become a homewrecker. But you are also naïve.

Suddenly, you are being paid attention to. You may feel that you are floating on air. You cannot believe that a man so powerful as him is considering you (naïve and fresh as you are) attractive enough to pay attention.

But understand that this is precisely why he is doing this. You are not wise enough. You are too emotional. He would never dare try this on an intelligent woman because she will immediately rebuff him. She knows how to protect herself. She values herself and her life and will never settle for a married man. She knows what sort of man she wants.

Consequences of your actions

You are reduced to waiting for a phone call.

You do everything stealthily.

Your social activities have come to a halt since you want to be available whenever he calls.

You are losing your friends.

Your goals are gone. It is all about him.

If he sees you on the road with his family, he will not give you the respect of acknowledging you. You are living with a man who is ashamed to be with you in front of his relatives! Is that your self-worth?

He will enjoy all the festivals with his family while you will be sitting in a lonely apartment with your life on hold until he calls again

You have become a lonely woman.

You have become a very unhappy woman

You are reduced to a woman with no self-respect. You tell lies to the ones who care most about you, your family. You may be driven to drinking or suicide.

He is ruining your life by his selfishness.

You may accept his offer of an apartment and expensive gifts. These are the prelude to becoming a high-class prostitute. No other man will look at you now.

You have nothing to protect yourself. Your children have no father.

You may end up marrying your boss.

Are you so low as to want a relationship over the broken heart of his spouse?

How do you know that he will not repeat the performance with someone younger than you after some years?

The only thing that governs a man's actions is his moral views.

Obviously, he does not have them, or he would not have broken his first marriage nor cheated on his wife.

How would an honorable man act?

If he had any honor, he would have said, "Please stay away from me. I am married. If I ever get divorced, and if you are still interested, I will contact you."

What about you?

Water attracts its own level. If you think that this is all you deserve, you will accept it. But if you value yourself, you will seek a mate who can go forward with you to build a life together.

Marriage means that he acknowledges you before society and *proudly* proclaims you to be his other half. Marriage means that he agrees in a written contract that he is responsible for your welfare and half of what he owes belongs to you and that he will be faithful to you.

Those women who think it is modern for them to have relationships without marriage are only fooling themselves.

Every man is grateful to them for believing so.

Because only then can he get what he wants with no strings attached and no consequences for his actions. So, who is dumb here?

Do not fall for the suggestions made by movies that being attracted to someone means that you jump into bed with them. Attraction is by your head. Jumping into bed is the other end of your body. Your head is what prevents your life from being ruined.

Value yourself enough not to lose your self-respect. Value yourself enough not to go to bed with anyone until you are married. Stay away from entanglements so that you have no baggage when you do meet the single man meant for you. Since you have done nothing to be ashamed of, you go forward with a clear conscience.

If you keep your moral boundary, the payoffs are great. Being monogamous does lead to peace and happiness, and you do not carry emotional baggage into your future.

Remember that it is not the way a man smiles or looks into your eyes that makes him good marriage material. It is only his character that will determine a happy outcome.

CHAPTER 10: THE QUALITIES NEEDED FOR WORK

I. How to speak (This is described above).

2. Appearance

3. Attitude

4. Focus

5. Ability to follow instructions.

6. Time management

7. Respect for your employer

8. Protection of the office

9. Character

10. Manners

11. Communication

12. Ability to handle criticism

You must maintain these standards and behaviors throughout your employment. Do not simply stop when you feel comfortable or settled in the workplace. Do not change your dress code.

1. How to speak

This has been described in the previous chapter

2. Appearance

Be neat. It is necessary to follow the dress code of the place you will be working at. You do not have to wear expensive clothes, but you should be clean and neat. You cannot just roll out of your bed and go to work.

You should have washed your face, hands, and feet and preferably taken a bath. Your clothes should not smell or be wrinkled. Your hair should be combed and tied back neatly, not falling all over your face. You should not be wearing slippers to work or high heels but low pumps. Women should not show their cleavage or breasts, wear tight skirts or short ones exposing their thighs. Men should not show their underwear. Do not hang your tie loosely around your neck. Your clothes are not supposed to distract others from the work you are doing. Avoid excessive jewelry. One bracelet, one neck chain, or one ring is more than enough.

The appearance of your workplace on leaving should be neat as well.

Do not fill your workplace with pictures of your family and friends. This is a place of work, not the library in your home. One picture is enough.

Papers should not be lying around. Unless it is urgent, do not start the next project before you have completed it and put away the first project.

Food should not be lying on your table. Finish your lunch, clean the table, and then go to work. When you leave, your working area should be clean.

3. Attitude

A. Attitude toward work:

Do you value work? Are you working just to pass the time?

Do you value your work as much as you value your family?

Do you want to offer excellence? This means that you could not do the work any better.

Do not be arrogant if you are being taught. Do not say that "I already know this." Just listen to the trainer.

B. Attitude toward customers:

Be friendly, helpful, and respectful. Be cheerful. Do not look depressed or irritable. Smile when you see someone. Leave your personal problems at home. You cannot excuse your behavior on the grounds that you are "having a bad day."

4. Focus

You are being paid to focus. Focus on what you must do. If you sign the wrong papers, write down the wrong appointment, or spell the name wrong, you cannot be excused for this. Do not take the wrong phone number. Repeat the number to the customer. Read back the spelling of the caller's name.

Check every detail again before showing your work to your boss. Make sure that you have completed all of it. There is no excuse for having dealt with five files but left the sixth one out or making three phone calls but not the other two. There is no excuse for carelessness.

You cannot hide behind the sentence, "I have no reason for what I did," or "It was an accident." What you are really saying is that either you did not care, or you deliberately disobeyed orders. In either case, you should be fired.

Understand that if you forget to do things, then you should expect some sort of professional reprimand.

Do not say:
"I forgot to do my routine,"
"I forgot to sign/date my message,"
"I forgot to pass on the message."
And never say, "I forgot to do what you told me to do." This is why you are supposed to write down all the details of the assignments given to you.

5. Follow instructions

Overconfidence and arrogance are the main factors in not following instructions. If you feel that you know how to do things better than your boss, you should leave the company before you are thrown out. Even if you feel that you are incredibly good at what you do, you forget that each company operates according to its own set of norms and standards. What works well in one does not necessarily do so in the other.

Second, your employer knows better than you as to what his company needs and in which direction, he is taking it.

Third, there are many reasons why he is doing what he does. If you knew the reasons, you would probably follow his instructions, but he does not have to explain them to you.

Fourth, your boss must trust you to keep you. If you do not follow his instructions, why would he trust you?

6. Time Management

Be on time. Do not leave early. If 8.30 is your starting time of work, you are to be at your desk by then. You should have taken off your coat, put away your things, go to the bathroom, and have eaten whatever you wanted to eat. That means you come in earlier than 8.30.

Do not leave early. If the office or store closes at five, you must be prepared to stay for one hour or more afterward. You cannot leave until the work of the day is finished and you are prepared for the next day.

A. The work for that day is finished when:

The boss has been informed of anything urgent.

The accounts have been reconciled, all files and things put away, and all machines refilled.

You have marked the supply list for things needed.

The office is neat and clean.

You have closed the curtains and cabinets and locked the doors (and whatever else the protocol of your workplace demands).

B. You are prepared for the next day when:

You have a list of things to be done the next day.

Your calendar has dates noted for important follow up.

All files are ready, appointments confirmed, and necessary phone calls made.

All items needed for the next day are brought out, place sanitized (and whatever else the protocol of your workplace demands).

If you are taking a day off, give the request in writing. Do not just casually mention it to your boss.

If you are sick, a doctor's note is needed unless your boss has excused you.

Work ethics dictate that you give two weeks' notice when you quit.

7. Respect your employer

Do not be rude to your boss. Do not badmouth your boss. Do not fight back. If you feel contempt or anger towards your boss, it will show up in your eyes. Look down. Excuse yourself and go to the bathroom and do some pushups to distract yourself. The key is a distraction. You can always replace one emotion with another by focusing.

If you want to show your employer that he cannot mess with you, then you are suffering from a bad case of inferiority complex and arrogance. Who wants an employee like that? Your boss wants someone who respectfully follows instructions. Do not confuse arrogance with self-respect.

Do not say, "But you also do the same." This is rude and conveys the message that you do not have much experience working in the professional field. He did not hire you to do what he does. He has different priorities and much greater responsibilities.

8. Protect the office

If you see a problem, take care of it, or call your boss. Your employer must be informed immediately of things that need urgent attention or repairs.

Never say that something is not your problem. A problem affecting the workflow of your office will eventually affect you.

Critical things must be put away before you leave, whether a medication, a syringe or a file.

Do not leave urgent messages on the desk of your employer, hoping that he will come to the office and check them. Phone him or send him an email.

Do not allow people to walk in and check the office, pick up material or copy files without informing your boss.

9. Character

You will be fired for lying or stealing. Keep your word. Do not say that you will do something and then not do it. Do not ever say that you meant the opposite of what you said to the boss.

You should be respectful, honest, dependable, responsible, and conscientious. Do not be lazy or procrastinate. It goes without saying that if you lie, cheat, and steal (items or customers), you are not going to be kept. Do not tell a boss that you lied to protect him or avoid hurting him. Once trust is broken, it cannot be given a second chance. Your character is on trial here. Follow your moral principles, and people will respect you for them.

Do not flirt with your employer or employee.

10. Manners

Read the section on "Manners at Work" in this book.

Look at the person when you talk to him/her. Do not look at your work or keep working and say, "Can I help you?" to the person at the window.

Do not use curse words.

Do not assume that you know what the customer or your boss is going to say and interrupt him. Let him finish.

Do not hit a person out of habit while talking to him.

Do not be arrogant with your colleague.

Do not sing at work unless everyone is doing physical work.

Do not talk loudly while your colleague is on the phone.

11. Communication

Ask if you do not understand your instructions. Ask if something in the office does not make sense.

Do not give messages to the boss on scraps of paper. Use an efficient system. Give messages when he first comes in and before you or he leaves, and in between if urgent.

Confirm with him that he has received the messages before you leave. People may not have had time to check their emails.

Do not ever make promises for your boss, "He will call you back." Say, "I will give your message to him."

Do not leave the customer on hold while you look for his file or seek an answer from your boss unless it is urgent. Ask the customer to call you back after a specific interval.

Do not walk into the office of your boss whenever something is bothering you. *You are distracting him.* Do not go with three things when he asked you to bring five. Collect everything and review it at the same time.

12. Accept criticism graciously

It is the person with an inferiority complex who cannot handle criticism.

Read the chapter on criticism in this book.

CHAPTER 11: WORK IN DETAIL

Work is the ability to offer excellence and to show others what you are capable of.

General Rules to Follow

What you do not value you will lose, whether it is your work, money, marriage or your files.

Do not reinvent the wheel. Learn what works from other people. That prevents you from wasting unnecessary time.

When your day starts, realize that you must first prioritize.

Phone calls first if possible.

Follow the acronym S.O. R.E.A.C.T. (See below).

If you are needed at work in an emergency, or if your boss asks for help, you should go to work.

Turn your cell phones off at work.

Keep your workplace neat and organized.

Keep your word. If you say you will do something, do it.

If your boss is giving you instructions, do not look around for someone else to do them. You have to do them.

Try to do things in the same order. That way, you have less chance of forgetting them.

Do a thing then and there while it is fresh in your mind, or else write it down.

If you value your time, you will make a list of things to do.

Check that everything is working before you start work.

"Finish a project before you go to the next project."

Finish a project and put away all items belonging to that project *before* moving to the next one. Do not have papers or things of your previous project lying around as you tackle the next project.

Do your homework before a meeting. That means to prepare for the situation ahead, what questions you will be asked and what materials you will need.

When you show the boss your task,

prepare for the questions he will ask!

Do not just walk out the door when your office time is over.

First, go over your list of what to do before you leave.

Look back when you leave a place to see that you did not leave anything behind.

A. Protocol

There is a protocol to follow when you come in, while you work and when you leave. There is also a protocol to do the work. Here are some guidelines to determine if you are accomplishing this.

B. Triage your work

Ask what the priority is in the work that you have been given when you first come in.

C. Plan your work

Have a list of the projects you must do that day so that you can mark them off as you complete them.

D. Phone calls

Unless there is something urgent, always do phone calls first.

First, finish the urgent calls of the day instead of other less time-sensitive work.

Then attend to the unfinished calls of the previous day.

Always finish the calls you left a message for on the previous day.

Return calls from your customer the same day.

E. Other work

Write down what you cannot do then and there. Post the list and check it frequently.

If you have a meeting scheduled later in the day, be fully prepared before it starts. Never run around looking for information after the meeting begins.

Finish the urgent work of the current and previous days.

Finish the work of the week that week.

F. Do not delay

Do not do things that delay you.

Write what has to be done for next week or must be followed up in your calendar.

Mark the work that is urgent and tell your boss about it before you leave.

Do not waste time. Finish the work on time.

G. Food

Eat at a fixed time at a designated area and not at your desk unless permitted to do so. Do not keep running to the kitchen to get a bite to eat every so often. Not taking lunch because you must work does not impress anyone. It shows that you do not care for yourself, which is unacceptable.

H. Be neat and organized

Neatness, organization, and working fast are keys to success.

Be neat and organized in your appearance, your desk, and your work.

Your boss should be able to find your work when you are gone.

Your boss should be able to see what you have completed and what you have not.

Write down what you must do and highlight what you have finished.

File things where they belong. Do not put charts or papers in the wrong place because you are in a hurry. Do put your files on the computer in the right place.

Do not write on loose scraps of paper.

If you have finished your work, look around to see what else you can do.

I. Before you leave

Before you leave, the work of the day should be put in its proper folder.

Calls or work uncompleted are flagged.

The next day you must follow through with those people whom you could not contact the previous day. You must also finish the uncompleted tasks of the previous day. Of course, you will do whatever is urgent first.

Do not leave until your list is flagged and everything is put back in its proper place.

Leave the list for the next day's work and follow-up calls in a conspicuous place where others can find it.

Keep your desk and computer organized so that if you do not come the next day, your colleagues can find your work and finish it. There should be minimal disruption because of your absence.

Look back to see that you have not left anything behind, and you have left the place clean and neat.

J. If you cannot come the next day, the following must be available:

1. Have the list for the next day's urgent work.

2. Have a list of the follow-up calls in a conspicuous place.

3. Have a list of the current projects on which you are working.

4. See that important business information is passed on to the next person.

5. Ensure that there is someone to open the business or order essential supplies.

Do you?

Do you have to be reminded of your tasks because you will not write them down?

Do you finish the work of the week, that week, and urgent work that day?

Do you have files and papers prepared for the next day?

Do you always have an excuse as to why you did not do the work?

Do nots

Do not say, "No one is helping me." You are supposed to be able to do your job by yourself. But if you are overwhelmed, let your supervisor know.

Do not mix your work with that of your colleague in the disguise of helping.

That is how you avoid responsibility because now the boss does not know who did what.

Do not follow orders blindly. If something does not make sense, question it.

Do not do a thing blindly. e.g., making copies without seeing if they are coming out properly or making a file without seeing if you have all the information.

Do not say, "this is not my job," if you are given another person's job to do.

Do not change your seat without permission.

PART TWO: S.O. R. E. A. C. T

CHAPTER 12: THE ACRONYM: S.O. R.E.A.C.T.

It is not enough to *value* work. It is equally important to know how you *behave in reaction* to work. This has been summed up in the acronym "S.O. R.E.A.C.T."

Each letter in the acronym stands for something:

S: SPEAK; **O:** ORGANIZE; R: Relationships; **E:** Excellence; **A:** Appearance; **C:** Character and **T:** Time.

S: How you **S**peak affects your ability to keep a job.

O: Organize your work and day.

R: Value **R**elationships with your customers, your colleagues, your boss, and your juniors.

Relationships at work are important.

E: Value and offer **E**xcellence.

A: Value your **A**ppearance.

C: Value your **C**haracter.

T: Value **T**ime.

Because of the time involved in each of these subjects, we will go over these backward.

VALUE TIME (REACT)

T stands for *Time.*

Do not waste your time or other's time.

Be on time. Staying late at work does not permit you to come in late.

One is punctuality, while the other is dependability.

59

Stay the time allotted. Do not keep saying that you have to come late or leave early. If you are the owner of a company, be in the office at a fixed time. Be physically present, overseeing all details.

Do not take excessive days off.

Do not keep saying that you are not well. Take time off to recover completely and then come back to work.

Do not rush out the door the moment your shift ends if something needs to be finished urgently.

Do not ask to leave because you have finished your work. Your work ends at the time allotted to you unless your boss has decided otherwise.

Finish the work on time.

Have a time limit. How long are you going to tolerate unfair work conditions at your job or home?

VALUE CHARACTER (REACT)

C stands for *Character*. It also stands for *Cleanliness*.

Do not only keep your desk clean but also help keep the office clean.

Keep the environment outside your office clean.

If your parents do not care about the trash outside your house, you will not care about the trash in and outside your building. Garbage causes diseases and epidemics. It affects wildlife and pollutes the earth. "Growing up" means to care about the welfare of animals and to care about the wellbeing of your planet.

Do not throw trash anywhere except in a container. If you see garbage outside, pick it up and dispose of it in a container.

Advanced societies are always known for their cleanliness, and their citizens are the ones that keep it clean.

Character-wise, it goes without saying that you are honest, dependable, responsible, conscientious, fair, and hardworking.

Do not underestimate yourself. You, as an employee, are the backbone of the place. You remove chaos, attract customers, and make the work pleasant. Your employer becomes helpless without you.

Being dependable, you keep your word and mean what you say. That is a relief to everyone.

Please do not say that you will do something and then not do it at the office, outside, or at home. Also, do not say that you meant the opposite of what you said.

But if you are respectful and without arrogance. You do not waste time nor things. You are not lazy, nor do you procrastinate. On the contrary, you are friendly and helpful. Your employer is lucky to find someone like you.

The fact that you do not malign the character of your colleagues or competitors, but protect their reputation, shows that you are comfortable with yourself.

You have the courage to be accountable for your mistakes. To say that you are sorry, acknowledge that you made a mistake, resolve that it will not happen again, and be willing to atone for it, are signs of good character, even greatness.

One will be fired for lying or stealing. You are trustworthy and not swayed by greed. No one would not dare offer you bribes to do the work that you are supposed to do.

If a work assignment is immoral or causes cruelty to people, we know that you will refuse to do it. You know your moral boundaries. However, a worker can be affected by the morals of his leader.

But there are those who abuse their wives at home. Their character at home cannot be separated from work. If you are a cheat or if you abuse your spouse at home, then you should not be kept at work. Your character will affect your behavior with juniors. Besides, the very fact that you are hiding your behavior at home from your office shows that you practice deceit and cannot be trusted.

A man cannot say that you should judge his work, not the way he conducts his personal life, because his character is intertwined with work. He must be judged on both aspects.

VALUE APPEARANCE (REACT)

A stands for Appearance. Steve Jobs, the maker of the iPad, laid a lot of emphasis on the appearance of his product.

Your workplace:

Your workplace should be neat, clean, and organized.

Your product:

Your product should be presented well.

Your appearance

Your aura, dress, and speech should reflect your professional attitude.

Aura

Your aura is how you come across. You should be cheerful, smiling, enthusiastic, confident, respectful, and helpful. Be neat. Be cheerful. Do not look depressed or irritable sorrowful, angry, or arrogant. Leave personal problems at home.

Dress

If you take pride in how you dress, it shows that you value yourself.

Appearance means that you not only follow the dress code but that you dress modestly. Dressing immodestly is also a sign of an inferiority complex. You are revealing your body to hide your lack of personality. Do not dress in tight clothes or show your cleavage, back, thighs or buttocks. Do not have thin straps instead of sleeves. Men should have neatly trimmed facial hair. They should not come in shorts or sandals. Clothes should be clean and pressed, not wrinkled. Appearance also means that you are clean and neat, your hair combed, and your shoes polished.

People meeting dignitaries or attending formal functions should not wear casual clothes or jeans. When you dress as expected for the place or occasion, it shows that you respect the feelings of your hosts and society.

VALUE EXCELLENCE (REACT)

E stands for *Excellence.*

You take pride in your work.

When you value excellence, you do not allow yourself to be distracted. Instead, you focus on your work.

Excellence means that you could not have done your work any better, and your colleagues do not need to complete or correct your work.

VALUE RELATIONS (REACT)

R stands for *Relationships.*

This is difficult for a few people. Some people can get along with their colleagues, but they rebel against their superiors. Some are difficult managers and cannot get along with their juniors. See where you fit in. No one is asking you to be a sycophant. No one is asking you to win a popularity contest. Do not be rude to your colleagues or your boss or fight back. You are not supposed to cry when you did not get your way or walk around with a glum demeanor because you were scolded. That is childish behavior.

General guidelines for valuing relationships.

Treat others as you would want them to treat you.

Smile at them. Do not be rude, even in fun.

Be cooperative and helpful.

Do not try to make others feel sorry for you

Do not do anything to embarrass others or make them uncomfortable.

Be considerate.

Do not disturb people when they are concentrating.

Do not say that you cannot help it if your voice is loud. Instead, move away to talk.

Be diplomatic in how you point out one's fault.

Let him "save face."

Do not counterattack if someone complains about you. Instead, apologize if you were wrong.

Refuse to join those who gang up against a colleague. Instead, make your own decisions after carefully thinking about the morality of the issue.

Do not ever succumb to a "mob mentality."

Do not embarrass your student in front of his family. Do not question his knowledge or make fun of it in front of his family.

If you need to correct someone, do it only twice. That is enough. Why waste your energy and make an enemy? If he is wrong, he will find out sooner or later.

The person who is an abuser at home can be very charming at work because he has the confidence that comes from financial and social freedom. But he is also sizing up people to see how much he can fool them or take advantage.

On the other hand, the one who is abused at home is timid. Up to now, her statements have been received with mockery and insults at home. As a result, it has been a long time since she has relaxed, talked, and laughed freely. However, this can change if she was not abused before the age of fourteen (depending on the degree and type of abuse). I that case, she can be quite charming once she overcomes her timidity and regains financial independence.

Get along with your customer.

Value your customer and treat him with respect and helpfulness. Do not make fun of him after he leaves. Do not lose your temper when he loses his.

Go the extra mile for him. Show him excellence. (See the do-nots in how not to aggravate a customer).

Get along with your colleagues.

Help your colleague if he is overwhelmed. You are part of a team.

Give credit to all the people who contributed to the work.

Be fair and treat others how you would want to be treated.

Remember that it is difficult for a bully or an abuser to get along with others.

Do not embarrass a colleague. Do not talk sarcastically.

Do step into your colleague's shoes for a moment and understand why he is saying what he is saying.

Get along with your boss.

Treat your boss with respect.

Do not rebel against authority.

Do not look at him with contempt. He can see it.

Do not decide that you know more than him or that you will put him in his place.

You are not here to fight with the establishment.

Do not criticize or make fun of him behind his back to others. The news will get to him.

Do not try to change the workplace.

You are here to make his work smoother, not to change it.

An employee cannot insist that he should do things his way unless someone's health or life is endangered. He should follow orders even though he thinks that the boss is wrong. The boss will eventually realize that he was wrong

Do not be too friendly with your boss

Do not talk to him about your personal problems.

Do not tell your employer that something in his appearance or aspect is bothering you.

Never tell an employer that it should not bother him if you take time off since he is not going to pay for it.

Do not go behind his back to his superiors unless you are being treated unfairly. Use the proper channels. If you do go behind him, do not state your case with emotion. Maturity is to state the facts calmly.

An employee cannot say that he forgot because he is supposed to write down what he needs to remember.

An employee is not equal to the boss.

He cannot retort to his employer that "you also do this." He does not do the other duties of his boss, face the extra pressure the boss must handle, take his risks, nor understand why the boss does this.

He must not confidently give an answer without checking his facts. It is the easiest way of losing the trust of his boss.

An employee cannot say 'okaaay" or "I get it" in order to shut his boss. Not only is it rude, but it shows his inability to listen and learn.

You were hired to make your boss's work easier, and his company's work run smoother. His confidence and trust that you are helping him and protecting the office should increase every day. He cannot do this if you treat him with disrespect or think that you know how to run the projects better than him.

You may not be allowed to do things the way you want to or the way you could in your previous company. Accept that. Prove your worth to him for six months before you want to ask for any changes and accept that you still may not get them.

Get along with your juniors

Be even-tempered. You are the one who sets the tone for the office atmosphere. Come in calmly every day. Let not your employees say, "The boss is so unpredictable.

One day he comes in with a smile. The next day he is angry and refuses to acknowledge anyone." So, everyone watches you nervously every day. You are not supposed to be at the mercy of your emotions.

Everyone, from the senior-most to the junior-most employee, should get the same friendly greeting from you.

Your juniors make your work easier, so you must value your staff. At the same time, keep your distance from your juniors. Do not discuss your misgivings or your private life with them.

Do not discuss one employee with another employee.

Do not insult a secretary by asking another employee in front of her. if what she said is true.

Never show favoritism to a new employee over your old employees or your family members.

Do not take out your anger at one person on another.

Do not show partiality to any worker because of his race, place of origin, ethnicity, because he works better, or for any other reason. Treat everyone fairly.

Treat people with consideration over what is happening in their lives.

Be clear about job descriptions.

Do not keep changing the instructions for the same work unless the need arises.

Be realistic in your instruction. They cannot do a three-hour job in thirty minutes.

Never ask your employees to do what you would not be willing to do yourself.

Even if it is their fault, do not blame them for an error in front of a customer.

Take the blame yourself and apologize to the customer.

Read the do-nots of scolding your employees in this book.

Scold your juniors privately. Do not embarrass them in front of others. But if it is something that you need everyone to be careful about, then you should discuss it in front of other workers calmly and professionally. There is a difference between shouting at an employee and telling him in a low tone that his behavior is unacceptable. Do not allow anyone to laugh when you are criticizing one employee.

Once you have been angry, get over it as soon as you can and start acting normally with them again.

Accept the fact that they will make mistakes. But they should not repeat them. Be willing to teach them and help them. You need to build a strong foundation. Remember that constant criticism drains the morale and enthusiasm of an employee and affects his work performance. If you criticize one day, then keep quiet for the next few days.

Encourage them and praise them at times.

You should be approachable. Listen to what they have to say and what they need.

Your employee should be able to tell you, without fear, if he thinks that you are wrong.

BE ABLE TO ORGANIZE (SO)

Have your files organized. Organize your routines on coming in and on leaving. Know when to take care of the work pending from the previous day and organize the priority of the work of today. Set the time for phone calls and the time to work uninterrupted. Have the list of work to be done tomorrow.

VALUE SPEECH (SO)

The way you speak shows your culture.

It shows your manners.

It shows your self-control.

Read chapter 2 titled "The tone of your voice."

If your colleagues call on you to help and you say, "no" you should be fired. There is no room for rudeness in the workplace.

Do not gossip among your coworkers while the customer is standing in front of you.

Do not criticize one customer to another customer.

Do not criticize your colleague to your customer.

Do not show that you have more knowledge or are more intelligent than others or that they are slow in learning. There is to be no contempt or arrogance.

Do not be aggressive and be ready to fight. ("Why is someone calling me? Can I have lunch in peace?").

If your voice is disturbing others, do not ever say, "This is the volume of my voice!" Move away to another area. Your consideration should supersede your arrogance.

Protect the reputation of others.

Do not speak badly about them behind their back, nor make fun of them.

Do not be a hypocrite.

Do not be nice to people on meeting them and then malign them behind their backs.

Bring people together instead of dividing them.

Defuse the situation.

Let us be tactful.

You do not have to insist that your opinions are right. Suppose someone said that bananas are blue. Why fight about it? There are other ways to say you do not agree:

Keep silent, or

repeat his sentence slowly or,

say, "Really? or,

Do you think so?" or,

"I do not know if I agree with that," or

"I am not sure if that is right," or

"Well, I'll be darned."

Suppose you are given a meal you do not like. Why say that it is terrible? Why not say, "It is different, or unusual, or too spicy or sour for me?"

There are many ways to address the situation.

PART THREE: FAMILY ORIGINS OF ATTITUDE

CHAPTER 13: SHOULD YOU PAY YOUR CHILDREN?

Parents who pay their children to do household chores are passing the wrong message. They, as part of the family, do their chores without being paid. If the children are to be considered part of the family unit, they too must do their share, and *no money should be paid for this*.

The children are a part of a family and should learn that all privileges come with responsibilities.

By everyone doing some work around the house, there is a deeper bond with each other and develop caring and consideration. The children are not "guests" who have to be served and entertained and who are doing a favor by helping. Quite the contrary, they will learn quite a lot by sharing in the workload, as you will see below.

If you had not worked at home

If you had not worked as a youth, if you had not done house chores when you lived at home, *you are at a disadvantage because you have not learned the "soft" work skills required at a job.*

You have not had the advantage of learning from people who have experience in work, your parents. You have not learned to work hard. You have not learned how to organize, make choices, stay calm, and make decisions when things suddenly go wrong. You have not learned how to innovate, be frugal, and not waste.

If you only work when you feel like working, then you have not developed a vital life skill called self-discipline.

Self-discipline means working when you do not want to. You have not learned that you must get up at a fixed time every day and that the chores must finish at a specific time every day. You have failed to learn that you cannot afford to be lazy.

When you do household work, self-confidence creeps in, which is so vital for survival. There is much that you can learn by doing household chores. These skills are reinforced when you work at a local business, but they cannot replace what you learn at home.

Fathers and mothers who, out of so-called love, do not require their boys and girls to do housework do their children a great disservice.

Mothers and fathers, who do not want their boys to do chores because they are boys, or do not want their girls to do chores because they are studying in a professional field, are not parenting properly. They are not allowing their children to develop skills and self-confidence.

There must be no fear

Children should be allowed to learn to do housework without fear of an adult's anger and without fear of being made fun of when they make mistakes. And they must be allowed to come up with solutions to their mistakes. These solutions may be wrong at first, but the children will realize that they are wrong and should correct themselves on their own. Wait until they ask for help.

CHAPTER 14: YOUR PARENTS AFFECT YOUR ATTITUDE

Your parents affect your attitude towards work. If your parent loved his work and showed his enthusiasm for it, it will spill over to you even if you hold a job different from his. If your father hated his job or was terrified of his career, you will unconsciously do so too. The good news is that you do so unconsciously, and once shown this fact, you can change your attitude. Even if one of your parents is a homemaker, her attitude towards work, and life, affects your attitude toward your career. The worst scenario is when your mother is abused and does her work in fear and pain, and your father hates his job and has contempt for his bosses. In such cases, it will help to find a mentor who can guide you. Here are some examples of what can affect you:

Perhaps your father abused your mother and opposed her every time she spoke. Now you get a sense of power by contradicting others.

Or your mother was timid, so now you may be afraid.

Your parents were prescribed anti-anxiety pills, and boy, do you need them now!

Your father works as a night watchman and is proud of his work and offers excellence. You have learned to offer excellence.

Your family has procrastinators, and you notice the same trait.

Marie Curie had to fight against people who did not think a woman should be in her profession. Yet, she had a love for learning. Is it surprising that Marie's daughter went on to win the noble prize? Her other daughter, Eve, too, fought against gender roles. She was a war correspondent during WW2 and reported from the front lines!

But consider the misfortune of the children born in a household where there are abuse and strife at home, where one parent is attacking the other. The children are too busy trying to survive and keep their sanity to absorb any work skills or the "soft skills." They need outside mentors to teach them. They need to go away from such a household so that they can calm down and be able to learn.

But you cannot resign to the fact that you are what you are because of your family. The brain is plastic. As an adult, you can learn from others, read books, take courses, and learn to correct your behavior.

CHAPTER 15: FAMILY INFLUENCES SUCCESS

Your family influences success but does not determine it.

Precursors of success can be determined just by knowing what sort of family you have. Did your family treat you with contempt? Did it foster self-confidence in you? If it did not, or if you had no family, did you have a mentor, or did the streets teach you to be confident? A lot can also be determined by whether you did chores at home, how your parents viewed their job, and how much selfishness there was in your home. Did your family teach you how to get along with people, or was it an antisocial family? In a "healthy" family, a child is surrounded by love and not made fun of. He likes himself and gains _self-confidence._

He must respect the boundaries of others, practice manners, and be considerate. He is taught to delay his gratification and handle frustrations. So, he learns _self-control._

The child has household chores to do. He works within time limits and structure. His room should be neat, and homework should be done within a fixed time. He learns _self-discipline._

He is required to mix with people of all ages socially (and not run into his room when "adults arrive)." So, he learns to be _social._

This is supposed to be the norm. Right?

But then there are other families where there are secrets. One abuses another. Perhaps there is addiction. Perhaps the child does not want to invite friends over as they may witness the bickering in his house. Or the parents are divorced, so the child is embarrassed for others to know. The child may be beaten or not permitted to play with others. In some societies, girls are made to hide in the back when adults visit; the result is that they become shy and feel inferior.

In such a household, there are some common attributes:

Children are not allowed to express their feelings.

No one cares about the child, what he does, and where he goes.

The child's efforts to succeed are mocked.

A girl is made to feel inferior because she is a girl.

The father has an inferiority complex. To compensate, he is hellbent on having all the power and will not allow the mother to teach the child anything.

Perhaps the child is taught not to think for himself but to follow blindly.

The family insists that if he wants to remain a part of the family, he must behave like a child, even though he is now an adult. He is not allowed to grow up.

He is not encouraged or given the confidence to attain on his own what he wants for himself.

The child may fall into addiction. He may have been put on medications for attention disorder and has become addicted to chemicals.

When a child is punished out of proportion to his misdeed, there are even graver consequences.

He was never shown to handle adversity and taught no spiritual strength, so at the first setback, he falls to pieces.

Despite all his degrees, how much self-confidence do you think this child will have on attaining adulthood?

The child may come from a poor family and has gratitude for the job and works hard. He may be from a rich family where money was not valued, and he was spoiled. He is not used to hard work, discipline, or responsibilities.

Now, this has nothing to do with your degree but has everything to do with how successful you will be. Millionaires have been reduced to poverty because of these traits. You may be thrown out of your job because of these traits. Your ultimate happiness and success may be affected because of these traits!

CHAPTER 16: THE OUTLIERS

In life, there are outliers to every norm. This is also true for people with their interpersonal skills. When people come from abusive families, they often become antisocial. They do poorly in work despite all their professional degrees. This is because they do not know how to interact properly with others.

In their homes, they were either ridiculed or shouted at. They were not invited to give their opinions. They spent long periods by themselves, so they lack social skills, which further complicates matters. Since they were not encouraged to chat or laugh, since they were treated "differently," they became quiet and awkward in their interactions. They were humiliated in front of others, which has made them shy. They were demeaned, so they feel inferior. They were treated with indifference even when they were ill, so they learned not to complain, even when it was right to complain. Since they only saw the behavior of the abuser versus the abused, they do not know how to treat people as equals. They are uncomfortable or suspicious when they are treated on an equal level. This suspicion may become paranoia later.

They cannot remember a time when they relaxed and laughed with others. When they go to school, their teachers consider them "different or difficult" but cannot understand why. The teachers see them being withdrawn or quiet, ridiculed, bullied, or fighting with each other. The outliers are not sensitive to the wavelength or pain of others.

This has ramifications in the workforce.

If the outliers do not care about your reaction, they will try to demean you or "teach you not to mess with them." If they care about your reaction, they will become submissive. Since they do not reveal their true feelings, it is difficult to get close to them. They are secretive people. When they advance to a managerial post, they cannot pick up the distress signals of their employees or when those junior to them are uncomfortable. They learn to put up an act of indifference to hide this.

Quite frankly, they feel as if they have landed on another planet where people behave differently from everyone they ever knew. So, they do not know how to blend in. Generally, they will stay away from society, not mixing with it, but existing by themselves. That is why they are dubbed antisocial. Because of their inferiority complex, they only associate with those whom they feel are on a lower level of society compared to them.

How do you undo this damage?

How do you change an awkward, fearful, shy, angry, and antisocial person, full of inferiority complex, into one who is relaxed, open, compassionate, friendly, confident, and who sees himself as equal to everyone? How do you give him self-value, self-confidence, sympathy, caring, and empathy?

Sometimes, this may not be possible in a lifetime, but we can try. The outlier must want to change. An outlier can learn by watching others and interacting with "normal" people, *but only when he does not feel arrogant towards them.* He cannot heed the advice of his spouse or relatives because he feels that they are inferior to him. Sometimes he can hold on to his job by being subservient.

Such a person does well in a job *where he does not have to interact with people,* as in computers, payroll, and other office work. He must be given small responsibilities at first and then advanced. He should be allowed to make a few mistakes and figure out the solution on his own. He must never be mocked for his mistakes. When he sees that his boss, whom he admires, treats him fairly and respectfully, his confidence is increased. Confidence is also obtained when he achieves small successes on his own and advances; or when he is appreciated by his colleagues and superiors for a job well done. Self-help books also help. What advances he makes has to be on his own, since he does not accept any guidance or a mentor.

These people do not do well at their jobs and are usually let go, not because they did not have the intelligence or that they were not hardworking, but because they could not get along. This is a waste of human potential.

PART FOUR: WHAT DO YOU NEED TO SUCCEED?

CHAPTER 17: THE VALUES NEEDED

What you do not value, you lose, whether it is your spouse, money, degree, or a job.

You must value yourself, and therefore your welfare, and have self-confidence.

You cannot work if you have an inferiority complex. Neither can you work if you do not have self-value, self-worth, and self-confidence. The most important qualities to possess are self-value and self-confidence. They can help when you are learning, working, or going through bad times in life. Self-value is different from selfishness. You know that you are good and have many qualities. Self-confidence is not the same as over-confidence.

Value the ability to support yourself.

You need to decide that come what may, you will support yourself, and you will work hard at it. If you make a mistake and are corrected, you will learn from it.

Value time.

Do not waste it. Do not waste your life.

You need to value work.

Be grateful for work. Value your workplace and work events.

Value physical health.

If you do not rest or eat adequately, you will be too sick to work.

Value mental health.

You cannot work if you are distracted, if you are in pain, or if your mind is clouded with chemicals or medication.

Value emotional health

You cannot work if your emotions are controlling you.

Value social health

Having friends makes all the difference in life.

Value your character.

If you are dishonest and selfish, you will not last long in the workplace.

Value self-control and self-discipline.

Self-control means that you do not do what you want to do.

You want to eat that piece of cake, but you will not.

Self-discipline is the opposite. You make yourself do what you do not want to do. You do not want to get up at 6 AM every morning, but you make yourself do it.

Self-discipline is crucial for success.

You may work in fits and starts because you have no self-discipline. You may go to work at different times. You may or may not finish your projects on time. You are at the mercy of your emotions!

It requires self-discipline to be at the office at the same time every day, to finish your work before you leave, to prepare for the next day, to prioritize, to do your homework before a meeting, to pay your bills on schedule, or to send your reports when promised.

Self-discipline comes into play when you force yourself to do what you do not want to do. It gives you mastery over your feelings, and you come out stronger.

Value your faith.

It will sustain you when all else fails.

Value others.

> Show manners. Manners mean consideration and respect for the other person and his values.

Manners do not mean only "thank you and please." Manners and respect are not meant only for strangers. They are vital for those you work with and live with. Your arrogance prevents this. Your inferiority complex makes you feel superior only when you demean others.

Value interpersonal skills. They affect your life profoundly. It is the difference between a life full of unhappiness and happy life. You need to get along with others at work and at home. This is not difficult if you come from a family with good interpersonal skills.

> But what if you came from a family with poor interpersonal skills, one that is rife with non-caring, demeaning, insulting, and selfish behavior?

Then this is an urgent "wakeup call" for you to realize that you have no interpersonal skills! You should find the guidelines for good interpersonal skills as soon as possible to avoid lifelong pain to yourself and others. Read about interpersonal skills as part of the chapter titled "S.O.-R.E.A.C.T."

CHAPTER 18: REMOVE YOUR INFERIORITY COMPLEX

Do not judge yourself by your failures.

Acknowledge the fact that God is not capable of making anyone inferior. How then can you be inferior?

Stay around people who treat you fairly and friendly and who like you for yourself.

Become financially independent.

Make your own decisions, thus gaining self-confidence. Take charge of your life.

Stay away from those who say that you are no good and laugh at your attempts at success, who try to demean you, treat you with contempt, and tell you not to think but blindly follow them.

Do not be ashamed of your mistakes

So, you made a mistake. We all make mistakes. What is important is that you learned from your mistake and will do it the right way the next time.

Do not be ashamed when you do not know a skill. No one was born having these skills. Now is your chance to learn.

You will see that most people are not that bad. In fact, they are quite friendly and caring.

CHAPTER 19: HANDLE CRITICISM

The hallmark of a developed person is the ability to handle corrections and criticism. If you have an inferiority complex, you cannot handle criticism.

No one wants to keep an angry or rude personality, no matter how good he is as a worker.

The things you do not do:

Deny what you did, "I did not shout."

Counterattack your boss, "You shouted, not me."
Counterattack your boss on *something else*, "You treat us like children."
Attack the intelligence of your boss, "You misunderstood."

This shows that you do not have the courage to speak the truth and have no respect for your boss. Why would he keep you?

Do not speak at the same time as the other person, especially your boss (or spouse).

Do not fight back with, "You also do this." You are the employee. He is the employer.

Do not place blame on others.

Do not make confrontational remarks like, "Are you calling me a liar or stupid?"

Do not cry, "I am hurt by what you said." This is manipulative behavior.

Do not answer a question with a question, such as, "Why would I do that?"

Do not say, "Everyone makes mistakes."

What you do is:

Listen without interrupting.

Wait for twenty-four hours to respond. Say, "I would like to have some time to respond."

If you made a mistake, say, "I made a mistake. I apologize"

This will now be discussed in detail.

Criticism is a part of life.

You will be criticized, even though sometimes unfairly. How you react to it is vital for your happiness and ability to keep a job

You have only two options.

One is to resent the criticism and continue to have friction in your life. The other is to think about it and make the necessary changes. Then try it for a month to see if it works.

> Remember that the person with an inferiority complex cannot handle the slightest criticism and will tell his spouse or his juniors to shut up rather than hear a single word.

The more comfortable you are with yourself, the better you can handle criticism. You must not take it personally. You need thick skin to allow it to roll off your back. You cannot control what another person says or does, but you can control whether you take it personally. It is one thing to fume and brood about it but quite another to think about it and see if he is right. If he was right, or if you want to try a new way, you accept it gracefully, apologize and change. If you think he is wrong, you can still stay quiet or go back later to discuss the situation

A mature person does not fight back, brood and plot revenge, or go around for days depressed or angry. One of the facts of life is that you will make mistakes. No one is perfect. Apologize graciously without grumbling ("I only made one mistake"), keeping a sad or angry face, blaming others, or fighting back.

Learn How to Accept Criticism

Do not take it personally

Criticism is not an attack on your very being. It is an instruction on how you can improve. If you take it as an attack, the opportunity for improvement is lost. Why not, for a change, just hear what the other person is saying? Study his motive. Does he just want to rub your nose in the dirt, or is he saying something that may make your work go smoother? No one likes to be criticized. But why not demonstrate maturity and try doing things differently?

Listen without interrupting.

Never speak at the same time as your superior. It is rude to do so. You show that you are not interested in hearing what he has to say. Instead of calming him down, you are enraging him with your behavior. Since you are not listening to what he is saying, you will repeat your mistake in the future.

Do not argue.

It may be your impulse to deny or make excuses for what you are criticized. For example, "What about the time when you or the other person did that?" or "I am not stupid." But fighting back only exacerbates the situation.

Do not point the blame to another.

Nobody likes a coward.

Do not spread the blame.

Do not say, "I am not the only one who made a mistake. He also saw it. He also knew of it." Take responsibility. You hope that by pointing to others, you will be scolded less. Others' participation does not minimize your mistake. Have the guts to own up to your behavior.

Do not respond to criticism by remarks.

"I am not stupid." Are you suggesting that intelligent people make no mistakes?

Do not cry, "I am hurt by what you said."

This is a form of manipulation. Instead of acknowledging that you are wrong, you are trying to make the other person feel guilty for trying to correct you. This compounds your mistake.

Do not answer a question with a question.

Do not say, "Why do you think that I would do that?" This is counterattacking. You are now trying to attack your accuser and make him defend himself. It shows no respect. The fact that you acted wrong is enough.

Do not raise your voice.

What you should do in response to criticism is:

Acknowledge your mistake and apologize. "You are right. It is my mistake. I am sorry."

Resolve not to repeat it. "It will not happen again."

Quietly go about your work.

Even if you think that you are right, wait twenty-four hours before you go back to speak about this with your boss. By that time, both of you will have cooled down and had a chance to examine the situation from a different angle.

Never laugh when someone else is being criticized.

Perhaps you, as a boss, can resolve issues in a constructive, nonconfrontational way

Sometimes a *suggestion* works better, "Let us try it this way."

Sometimes a *statement* works better, "In my experience, it works best this way."

CHAPTER 20: HIERARCHY AT WORK

Equal rights pertain only to fundamental rights.

We know that under the law, we are considered equal, but this only applies to our constitutional rights. We cannot apply this logic to a workplace, corporations, institutions, military, or certain aspects of life. There must be a hierarchy for institutions to function smoothly, and you must accept that hierarchy.

A nurse is not equal to a doctor, and a nurses' aide is not equal to a nurse at the hospital. A secretary is not equal to her boss or other people senior to her in knowledge or position. A student is not equal to his teacher. A corporal cannot contend with a general and say, "I am equal to you, so I do not like the way you talk to me," or "you make me feel small when you talk to me like this." How you feel is entirely up to you. A person cannot tell his father, "I am equal to you since I am earning. So, I do not have to show you any manners." You cannot tell your senior, "I was on the phone first."

Whether we like it or not, there are people superior to us in the workplace and in life. It is immature not to realize this. This is well known in the private sector. Maturity is acknowledging that equality cannot be applied to a professional hierarchy, which must be maintained if work is to run smoothly.

You do not become small by showing respect to another person or giving him preference over your own interests. How you speak to those who are senior to you in position reflects on your family upbringing, manners, and culture

Respect those who are senior to you in age, rank, pay, position, knowledge, or experience. Treat your seniors with respect and politeness. Do not be too familiar with them. Do not make fun of them. Do not ask them to do your work. Do not tell them that their appearance bothers you. Do not cut them off when they are speaking by your words or gesture. Show them your good manners. This is not infringing on your rights as an equal human being. This is about etiquette. The two are separate.

CHAPTER 21: MANNERS AT WORK

Manners mean that you make the other person feel comfortable and respected.

Most of us have good manners and are pleasant to be around. It is good, however, to remember some points.

Competence without good manners, and a pleasant attitude, is unacceptable and shows a lack of upbringing and culture.

Having manners means that you have the self-control to behave in a way that your lower self does not want to. You have to eliminate selfishness.

Lack of manners shows that you have no self-control. You are selfish. It also demonstrates that you have neither respect for the other person nor regard for his feelings. People are not supposed to laugh at your rudeness. They have a right to feel insulted and hurt. They should feel pity for you that you have neither polish nor culture. They have a right to refuse to work with you.

Do not learn bad manners from television or other media. When someone asks you for something or for you to do something, do not say "no" or "I do not want to." Even if you are not going to do it, you should apologize and say that you regret that you cannot do it for the following reasons. If you agree to do something for someone, never complain about how inconvenient this is for you. Just because you gave assistance in the past does not permit you to be selfish in the present.

Do not chew gum at work when you are a white-collar worker, or are at an appointment, in a class, in meetings, functions, in a church or a temple, at a holy place, at a memorial service, at a funeral, or in front of a priest, teacher, a doctor or someone respected.

Manners mean that you allow a person senior to you in position, a woman, or the elderly to go into the room or elevator first. You should offer them your seat.

If you have been seated in a room, and the person you made an appointment with, walks in, stand up and greet him. This also includes your doctor and your child's teacher. Do not eat in front of him during the appointment.

How you speak is critical to having manners and creating a pleasant work environment,

There should be no profanity and no vulgarity. Do not be rude. Do not curse. This includes words like "shit."

What you say is indicative of who you are because the words are first made in your brain.

If you speak vulgarly, then it reveals you as a vulgar person.

If asked how he is by a senior, a junior person cannot say, "Not as well as you." Do not be passive-aggressive in your interactions.

Do not be over-familiar with your boss. Do not ask him if he had a good lunch. Do not call her sweetie if she is a woman.

Do not ever call a person by his first name unless he permits to do so.

Calling a person Mr. or Mrs., Miss, sir, or madam, is a sign of respect. Understand that people who have dignity always treat the other person with respect. What is dignity? It is self-worth. A person who secretly has an inferiority complex can only feel superior when he treats someone else rudely.

Do not speak with your back to the customer. Look people in the eye when they are talking to you. Do not keep working at such a time. It does not show that you are busy. It does show that you have no manners. Face the person whom you are talking to and give him your full attention.

Wait until the other person finishes speaking before speaking yourself. Television hosts are notorious for showing bad manners and cutting off a person before he finishes speaking, but you are not on tv.

Never say, "I was speaking first." Stop talking and say, "Please go ahead."

Do not be silent after the customer speaks, and then when he repeats himself, say, "I heard you the first time." How is he supposed to know that you heard him if you have not acknowledged him?

Personal development means that you treat everyone with good manners regardless of their wealth or power. You must also respect people who may have no money but have knowledge. Treat the elderly and your parents with respect because they have far more experience than you.

PART FIVE: THE "DO-NOTS" AT WORK

CHAPTER 22: THE "DO NOTS" IN SCOLDING YOUR EMPLOYEES

Your goal is not to demean your employee. Only a person with an inferiority complex does that. Your only goal is to see that this mistake is not repeated by him or others.

There is to be no sarcasm and no insulting. Your purpose is not to humiliate him verbally. There is a difference between saying, "You are a fool," and saying, "We do not accept such type of behavior," That does not mean that you cannot fire him.

Do not scold him again the next day. One time is enough.

To make an employee do "physical" punishment in a civilian office, such as push-ups or running around the block, only shows that you are not fit to be an employer and that you must be removed immediately.

Before you start, think of his overall performance and the contribution that he has made or is making. Also, consider whether this is a trait of his personality or a pattern of his behavior. And then think about how you will handle this.

Place and time:

The first time that you scold him, do so quietly, or in front of a disinterested party as a witness.

Do not scold him in front of others unless it is a rule that everyone must follow.

Do not scold him on a date that is important to him. It is his birthday or of someone else in his family or Christmas and so on.

Do not scold him when he is in fear or worry. For example, his wife is undergoing an operation.

Do not scold him for his failure on project A when he is trying to please you on project B.

Unless it is imperative, do not scold him in the morning. You will ruin his enthusiasm for the day. Stick to after lunch.

Do not scold him about two separate things at the same time. Stick to the problem currently in question.

Procedure:

Look at him when you talk to him.

Keep your voice low. Do not shout.

Even if an incident occurred in front of you and others, do not scold him then and there, in the heat of the moment. Try to do it by the evening or the next day while the incidence is fresh. Ask him to come into your office away from other colleagues.

Do not start by praising him. He should not connect praise with criticism. You cannot say, "You are always in time, but-."

However, later, or the next week, find something genuine to praise him about.

Be specific. There is a difference between "You are always late" and "For the past week, you have been clocking late. Can you give me a reason for that?"

Let him "save face" the first time.

Your punishment of your employee should not be done publicly. And it can never be out of proportion to the deed.

Document what you are doing.

CHAPTER 23 GENERAL RULES

If you are courteous and helpful, if you offer excellence and keep your word, you will not go wrong.

Do not shred your employer's reputation. Do not shred your colleagues' reputation.

Do not have the "don't mess with me" attitude.

Do not rebel for the sake of rebelling or power

Focus

Focus on your work. No one likes a careless worker. Do not write the wrong name or date, nor sign on the wrong sheets. You are supposed to focus on the job.

Do not repeat your mistakes after having been corrected.

Do not aggravate the customer.

Be professional. Do not call the customer "dear" or "sweetheart."

Never call your customers by their first names unless they permit you to do so. It can be considered rude by many. Calling someone Mr. or Miss only shows that you have good manners.

Do not show bad manners.

Do not be familiar with your customers. Do not discuss your private life. Do not ask prying or personal questions about the customer's life (whether she lives alone, what work does she do, etc.).

Keep your word. Do not quote a price, but after you finish the work, ask for more money.

Do not argue with a customer. Do not insist that it is his fault. Just see how you can correct the situation to his satisfaction.

Keep your personal conversation on the phone to the minimum possible when a customer is in front of you.

Do not say, "I have no idea," to a customer. Instead, see if you can direct him to the information. If you cannot get the information, say, "I am sorry. I do not seem to be able to get the information you need. If you could call me later, I may be able to find it for you."

Except in emergencies, or unforeseen circumstances, do not keep a customer waiting.

Do not make a customer come back for what can be done for him today.

Do not ever sit in front of a customer and refuse to help him because you are on "a break."

Do not ever tell a customer that he is the only one complaining about something.

Thank him for telling you that there is a problem and assure him that you will look into it right away.

Do not keep repeating yourself if a customer is trying to understand something from you. Repetition will not make a customer understand and increase his frustration. And it shows that you do not understand the problem. Instead, get your supervisor to help the customer.

If you, or the people you hired, made a mistake or damaged something, do not keep quiet. Call your employer or the customer immediately. Apologize and explain what you are going to do to correct the situation and when. If he is not happy with that, refund him his money. He will remember you for being honest.

> Do not discuss your moral, religious, and political convictions with your customers. This is neither the place nor the time to do so unless they ask you to violate your moral ethics.

Do not disturb others.

Do not be talkative.

Do not eat, sing, or pass remarks while working. Do not think aloud or talk to yourself.

Do not gossip near a person who is concentrating. Do not talk over his head with your colleagues.

Do not talk loudly and say that this is the tone of your voice and that you cannot whisper. The medical profession knows that this is not true.

Do not put the radio or music on at work unless everyone is doing only physical work.

People who are doing maintenance work, or bringing food to professional persons, are not supposed to gossip among themselves in the office area. Do your work quietly.

Do not disrespect your family

Never insult or demean your children or spouse to impress your colleagues. They will not be impressed. Rather, they will see that you are suffering from an inferiority complex, you do not have the wisdom to handle frustrations, and you are an abuser.

Never interrupt your boss.

Do not assume you know what the boss is going to say and start answering before he finishes speaking. Listen quietly and wait until he is finished, even if you know what your answer is.

When you are being trained on a project, do not interrupt or say that you know all this. Listen quietly. You may learn something new or a better way of doing things.

Do not aggravate your boss

Do not be nice to your customers, but rude to your boss.

Do not be nice to your boss, but rude to your colleagues.

Do not start speaking to him as you are walking to his office. He is focusing on his work.

Never call out to your boss from where you are sitting whenever you think of something. Get up and go to him.

Do not disturb your boss by running to him every time a thought strikes you. Make a list of all your ideas and needs for the day before seeing him.

When you give your employer his messages, start each one with the name of the caller and the company that he represents.

Do not tell your boss that you are ready for him to review your work, and then ask him to sit by and wait while you finish it.

Never present your work to your boss without checking it yourself and removing all the mistakes.

Before you show the boss your task,

prepare for the questions he will ask.

Bring all the reports and faxes at certain times.

Do not keep bringing one item at a time to your boss. If he gave you some work to do, keep it until he tells you to bring it, unless he asked you to get it immediately.

Do not tell your boss that you forgot to do the work that he assigned you. Do not compound your mistake by saying that "everyone forgets." If this is what you believe, then it should not bother you if your boss forgets to pay you since "everyone forgets."

The boss hired you, expecting you to be dependable and responsible. But in this scenario, you are neither.

Please note that your chances of forgetting are much less if you do things in the same order,

Do not say, "This is not my job."

Do not pass on the work that you were given to someone else to do.

You must have a routine of things to do in the same order when you come in and before you leave, whether it is taking messages, checking your notebook, and so on.

Do not try to surprise your boss by doing a project by yourself. If you have mishandled it, you have wasted his and your time. Tell him about your plan. Show him a sample to see if you have executed it correctly before continuing.

You should not complain about your boss to his superior unless it is a serious matter.

Do not speak thoughtlessly

Do you say a thing without checking if you are right? "The file is right there." If it is not, people will quickly learn not to trust you.

Your purpose is not to prove to your boss that you are right, and he is wrong. You are not going to be kept on for long if you do that. Though you say nothing to him, he will find out if you were right.

Keeping quiet and doing your work well can be more impressive and achieve much more goodwill.

Do not start talking about your requests or problems while handling any work with your boss. Tell him that you wish to schedule some time for yourself.

If your boss asks you about where a file is, do not ever say, "I gave it to you.". On the other hand, if you do not say that you gave it to him, but he later finds out that it is true, he will admire you for your tact.

Remove the words, "*you told me to do this, or you told me to put it there!*" It shows that you only want to fight. Similarly, it is one thing to repeat yourself once. "I gave it to you." But once you insist on a thing more than twice, you are showing that you want to fight. Your words should soothe, not irritate!

> If you have to say "no," see if you can say it without being confrontational and with the attitude of how you can help.

There is a difference between "No, I do not know where that is" and "No, but I can look for it or let me you help you find it."

If you are wrong or did not keep your word, please do not look for an excuse and do not lie if you wish to keep the other person's respect. You should be known for your honesty. Say that you are sorry, that it will not happen again, and ask what you can do to rectify the situation.

CHAPTER 24: EXAMPLES OF "DO-NOTS" AT WORK

Most of you are modest, decent, kindhearted, and hard-working people, the best. But sometimes, one comes across a person who may need to be tweaked. Hopefully, you do not recognize anyone in the examples given below.

Dress

You dress indecently. You show your cleavage, and your dress outlines your buttocks. Your skirt is climbing up your thighs, and you are going to attack the first person who tries to control your freedom to do so.

A woman's lack of clothing is an attempt to cover the fact that she has a lack of talent or personality. She has nothing else to attract a man except her breasts and her buttocks. But the workplace is not the area to show your inferiority complex!

A man should not keep his pants low to show his underwear. He should not wear shorts or sandals to work.

Attitude

Millie works hard and is pleasant to be around. But she is slow in her work. It takes her days to do what others do in one day.

John does not know how to prioritize. His desk is full of projects, and he does not know where to start.

Jack is lazy. He keeps putting everything the boss gives him in a tray. When the boss calls for his work, John says that he has been given so much to do that he could not complete it. The only way to handle John is to review his work twice a week, which is a waste of his employer's time.

James cannot organize himself. He does not know where his customer's files are. He forgets what calls he has to make! He has no system for tracking his assignments and progress. He tries to cover this by being friendly with the customers, but it still creates a lot of ill-will.

Jim was never taught to be neat as a child. His desk is a mess of papers into which he has to dive to look for things he wants. This wastes everyone's time. He does not put away the project that he has finished before he starts the next one. The day he fell ill, the office spent two days trying to find critical files.

Joe is hard working and good-natured, but he is trying to attract clients who he will steal as soon as he leaves the office.

Bob does his work half-heartedly. He always has an excuse for why he could not meet the deadline.

Bill constantly interrupts his work by talking to everyone and so loses his focus and distracts others.

Patty is always asking others to do her work.

Judy is furious when she is asked to help another colleague, "This is not my job."

George has decided that if he can suck up to his boss, he can climb up the ladder, no matter how he performs.

Mary decides that it is time for her to take a vacation. She does not care that the other worker is ill at home and that the boss has just come back after some days. She knows her rights.

Tina's face is full of sorrow because she had to leave her country to migrate here. She left all her loved ones back home. The customers feel uncomfortable around her.

Ruth is so depressed with life. Her husband has left her. The children are overwhelming. She cannot muster the enthusiasm to sell her company's product to a potential buyer

Sandra is in her own world. She is so befuddled that she signs her name on papers belonging to other people. Her documents are full of mistakes all the time, which enrages the boss. She refuses to check her work before she presents it to him.

Henry cannot wait for the clock to strike five so he can run out of the office. He refuses to stay to meet a deadline. His time was supposed to end at five.

When no one is looking, Peter runs out of the office for a few hours to enjoy himself.

Mark just got promoted to a manager's position. He has such a bad temper that people are scared to clarify instructions or ask questions.

Jill is asked to come back to the hospital because there is a sudden influx of patients. She refuses. After all, her shift is over. This is her family time, and she knows that her husband will be displeased if she goes back. Her marriage has priority over her colleagues' inability to cope with the situation.

Steve is so rude that his colleagues do their best to avoid him, but then how can they work on projects together?

Shirley feels that she is overwhelmed with work, so she has an angry face all day, every day, but she will not address the issue with her boss.

Brian feels that God made him equal to his boss so he can shout at him.

Barry's father said that it was okay to cheat and cut corners to survive. Brian believes a dutiful child should follow his father.

There is a position available, and everyone is ready to cut the throat of others so that he can grab it.

How do you treat others?

You, as a secretary, have decided to treat everyone equally. So, even if a colleague of your boss comes to see him, you yell at him to wait for his turn in the reception room.

You are a sanitation worker. You decide to sing as you clean around the office workers who are trying to focus on their projects and meet a deadline. This is not about consideration. This is about your rights as a human being!

You are a blue-collar worker. You see a computer available, and you sit down and start playing on it. Let the office-worker wait for his turn, even though he needs it for his work since God made everyone equal.

You see that your current company does not do what your previous company did to expand itself. You also

115

notice that what you were taught as an important strategy in school is not applied in your current company. So, you decide that your boss is an idiot. You look at him with contempt and criticize him to everyone whom you meet.

You work as a secretary in the hospital. You do not believe in a hierarchy and are going to be equally rude to everyone, regardless of their positions. So, even if you are a secretary, you are going to shout at the patients and doctors. This is how you get your kicks!

The doctor in the hospital is trying to concentrate on his report and you, the secretary, are shouting over his head to tell others that a funny thing happened to you this morning. When he protests, you mock him!" Doctor, have you no concentration? This is the tone of my voice, and I cannot lower it!"

Should we be famous in the world for having bad manners?

Does not television teach us that we can be downright insulting as long as we do our job well?

It is easy to be offensive because practicing no self-control and letting our base instincts rule supreme is always easier! Besides, it feels more powerful. But do you really value yourself when you do that? And it is not you who are powerful. Instead, it is your emotions who have you tightly in their control.

Thankfully, the majority are the following types of people, and thankfully, you are one of those.

They have self-respect, but they also treat their colleagues and their boss with respect.

There are people who value themselves but still follow the hierarchy of a company.

They dress and behave decently.

They are people who value their work and offer excellence.

They are people who will fulfill their responsibilities

They work within moral guidelines. They are people who will play fair.

They do not cheat or lie.

They do not take bribes to do their work.

They are patient, dependable, and efficient so that the company does not lose customers.

They focus on their work. They will ask about what needs to be prioritized today.

They will remember the customer they could not reach the day before and follow through.

They are polite and tactful. "Tact is the art of telling a person to go to hell in such a nice way that he thanks you."

They do not mind helping an overburdened colleague.

They can be friendly without being nosy.

These people are friendly but considerate. They will keep their voices low so that you can work. They will move away from you if they wish to chat with colleagues.

Their desks are neat and organized.

They will protect the office

They will innovate if necessary.

They are people the boss will want to hire again.

PART SIX: THOUGHTS FOR SELF REFLECTION

CHAPTER 25: QUESTIONS FOR SELF-REFLECTION

1. How are you as a person?

Are you timid/arrogant, depressed/cheerful quick-tempered/calm, or friendly/aloof?

2. Do you have self-value?

Or do you suffer from an inferiority complex?

3. Are you neat and clean?

4. How do you dress?

5. How do you get along with the people at work?

Can you interact well with your boss but not with your colleagues?

Can you interact well with your customers but not with your boss?

Are you a team player?

6. How do you react to criticism?

Do you take it personally and fight back? Do you sit and cry?

7. Do you accept hierarchy at work?

8. Do you value time?

9. Are you efficient or lazy?

10. Do you allow your personal life to affect your professional life?

11. Can you focus on the job?

Do you keep repeating your mistakes?

12. Are you a conscientious worker?

Will you do your job well even if no one is checking?

13. Do you start changing the way things are done once you are comfortable at work?

14. Are you honest?

Or do you enjoy making a fool of others?

15. Are you responsible?

16. Are you dependable?

Do you keep saying, "I forgot?"

17. How do you speak?

Do you defuse the situation, or are you confrontational? Do you soothe or irritate?

18. Do you increase the workload or decrease it?

Do people have to correct your mistakes? Do they have to enter things that you forgot into the computer? Do others have to clean up after you?

19. Do you file things incorrectly so that others waste time looking for them?

20. Do you make promises for other people?

An example: "The boss will call you at three pm."

21. How efficiently do you work?

Are you organized?

Do you write down what you need to do for that day and the next day?

Do you put away your finished project before starting the next one?

Do you finish the work of the week that week?

Do you prioritize?

22. Do you have the self-discipline, good manners, consideration, and self-control needed to work?

CHAPTER 26: WHAT SORT OF MANAGER SHOULD YOU BE?

You cannot be an angry person. If your juniors work in fear, they will make mistakes.

You should have the same daily smiling appearance. Do not have mood swings.

Keep a wall between you and your juniors while staying pleasant. There should not be over-familiarity.

Be hard-working yourself. You cannot be watching television while your employees are working. You must set an example. Pitch in when they are overwhelmed. Do not be afraid to get your hands dirty.

Be clear in your instructions. Never expect them to know what to do.

Do not keep changing your instructions.

Be a humane manager. Do not cut into your employee's family time at home or on weekends. A manager must be considerate.

A manager, or a boss, must be able to apologize to his employees for his behavior. He should also be the one who apologizes to the outsiders for the actions of his employees.

Never say, "I do not know how you will do it. Just do it."

A bully does that. You are paid more money because of your increased knowledge and experience. It is your duty to show your employees how the situation can be handled. That is what you are paid for. If they can figure out something that you cannot, then they should become your managers.

You must not show any partiality to your employees.

Know the "do-nots" in scolding your employees.

CHAPTER 27: REMEMBER!

Be clear on what you will or will not tolerate from anyone.

Show no impulsive behavior.

But do state when you are overloaded. Your work should be within your capacity.

What should you do if your superior does not approve your plan, but you, as an administrator, feel that it is vital for your institution? You must start looking for ways to work around your orders.

> Your personal development demands that you leave a job immediately if it is immoral or if it involves cruelty.

If you are faced with the dilemma of being asked to do something against your principles, you have two choices. You can speak up, refuse, and face the consequences, or you can see how you can work around it.

He is a wise man who does not bring the frustrations of his workplace back to his family. Once you cross the threshold of your house, be grateful that you have a family and meet them with a smiling face. Home is an equally important part of your life. Keep the feelings of your work, at work, and the feelings of your home, at home. This is a sign of wisdom.

There are children coming from families who tell them to value work, be a hard worker, and value money. They will do well.

There are children coming from families who teach them that money is dirty and not to value work. They have been allowed to do whatever they please. They have been allowed to be lazy. They will fail in work

A parent is an abuser if he insists that his grown-up child take the career that the parent wants for him and go to work in the country that the parent dictates.

A parent is an abuser if he insists that his child must not think for himself but follow his parent blindly, even if it causes pain. Such a parent is an enemy of the child. The child must get away from him to survive!

That a woman cannot work as well as a man, and therefore should be paid less than a man, is a myth propagated, of course, by men.

Man has always thought that his physical strength and financial power somehow seep into his brain and make him more intelligent.

Medical science shows that this is not true.

CHAPTER 28: REFLECTIONS ON WORK AND HOME

Man is a rational being. He uses logic to advance, yet sometimes, man fails miserably, and his selfishness overcomes all logic.

A man knows that he is taller than a woman. He is bigger. His bones are thicker, and his muscles are bulkier. All this would lead even a sixth grader to conclude that a man is physically stronger than a woman. Being wise, a man will never let a weaker horse do the work that he expects a stronger horse to do. Right?

Yet, let a man get married, and he loses his logic completely. He may have a job where he has sat the whole day at work. On coming home from work, he has the self-preservation to rest. But then he does not want to move at all! Yet, he expects his wife to come home from a similar job and immediately start cooking, cleaning, and taking care of the children and the house! Why is he conveniently forgetting that she has scientifically been proven to be physically weaker than him? Should this be considered selfishness?

What man would agree to let his wife come home and sit down in front of the tv, while he comes home from work and starts running around, cooking, cleaning, and taking care of the children? Why not one man? Because a man demands fairness!

You cannot demand fairness but be unwilling to reciprocate.

It is interesting to watch what happens when men share a house. They will strictly obey the division of chores and be fair. This is because each man has a high value of himself. He will not tolerate unfair treatment from another. So, what changes when one of these men gets married? Why does he start treating his spouse unfairly? And why does a woman permit unfair treatment? Does she not have a high opinion of herself?

A man's wife may not be working but is running around with the children and taking care of the house. He has worked all day. If he is physically exhausted, he should rest. But a man may not be exhausted. He will come home, have dinner, and then go straight to the gym. He does not think about helping his wife. Would he allow his spouse to do this to him?

> He goes to the gym to build up those very muscles that are not being used in helping his family.

You must give your wife the same consideration that you would want for yourself. Marriage means a division of labor and finances, as well as consideration and absolute fairness to one another. These must be agreed upon prior to the marriage.

If one collects the garbage, the other takes it out; if one cooks, the other cleans the dishes; if one does the laundry, the other folds; if one sweeps, the other mops. If one cleans one part of the house, the spouse cleans the other part. If a husband does not want to be disturbed when he is sleeping, then he should not disturb his wife when she is sleeping. If one wishes to be given tea and dinner on coming home from traveling, he should be willing to do so in return. If one is overcome with fatigue, the other should take over. If there are no children and the wife is not earning, she is still taking care of the house. He should help her with the cleaning and cooking over the weekend.

This must be regardless of how much each person earns.

Bones and muscles do not change in structure, depending on how much money you make. Ask any doctor.

Earning money does not mean that you should give up advancing in your development as a human being. You cannot develop if you are not fair or considerate. If you think that your wife is not really working (since she is not earning), hire a housekeeper and see how much you must pay for the same services!

Fortunately, there are many more men who are wiser, fair, and further developed. They do not get an inferiority complex by doing household work.

They extend to their spouse the same considerations they wish for themselves.

By doing this, they avoid the bitterness and resentment that can build up in an unfair marriage. Caring and consideration get more love. A deeper bond develops as you talk while you share your chores.

PART SEVEN: SHOULD YOU WORK WHILE IN SORROW?

CHAPTER 29: WORK WHEN YOU ARE IN EMOTIONAL PAIN

Value work, value money, and value himself!

You have had a loss. Your trust has been betrayed. You are drowning in pain. Your wife left you. Should you be working?

Though we are discussing work basics, it is important to digress and address the people who do not want to work because they have had a tragic life event. They are not lazy. They are intelligent people, but they are so overcome by their sorrow, whether from a divorce, a betrayal of trust, or a loss (including a loss of a loved one), that they have lost the motivation for work. This chapter is for them.

You must survive physically and emotionally to survive financially.

Physically

If you care for someone who is going through a difficult time, your main objective should be that he does not become self-destructive. A lot of energy is taken up by what he is going through. He has to heal. But he must survive physically first.

Wait for a month or so to allow him to go through the acute phase of the pain. In this stage, make sure that he is physically taken care of.

Since he is overcome by his emotions and/or in shock, logic cannot reach him at first.

Emotionally

One must find a reason to live, a purpose to go on despite what has happened.

> "He who has a *why* to live can bear almost any *how*." (Nietzsche).

Sometimes the purpose is in *how* you bear your cross or *how* you handle your suffering (Viktor Frankel).

It is important to remember that life is greater than what you have just been through. No matter how close you were to a few people in your life, there are others waiting to cross paths with you, and there are other experiences you need to go through to develop.

This finding of purpose may take weeks to years. In the meantime, one must start acting as if one has a purpose for himself or others and devote time daily in introspection. The first step in finding the purpose is to take care of yourself.

So, once he has calmed down, you must talk to him about the next step.

There must be a time limit to lying around crying to avoid self-destruction.

If he is distraught, he should take two weeks to two months off to seek healing *actively* and then go to work. He can then continue therapy after work.

It is important to go to work because the first two rules are not to be dependent on others financially and not to use up one's savings.

He should go to work, and he should succeed at work. He must summon his courage to survive each day.

The self-worth and self-respect that he may have lost in bad times, he will gain by working and supporting himself. It is good to be financially independent. He should offer excellence at work, even when he does not want to.

He may say that there is no goal to live for. He is the goal! He was sent here for a purpose. He may be comforted by the fact that he may be needed by his children in the future. He is helped by taking care of others who depend on him for survival and comfort.

"It is in giving that we receive."

There may be something that he can do in the name of the one he has lost. In any case, he should wait for life to turn a corner and see what else it has to offer.

However, he should understand that it is not enough to work. The first thing a customer looks at is you, not your work. This is a crucial point.

If the customer sees that you are in turmoil instead of being calm, in pain and suffering instead of peaceful, you have just lost a customer. So, it is imperative not to let your pain be apparent to anyone.

If you are the one who is suffering, know the following.

People may grow up and change their attitude to you if that is what is bothering you.

Your loss may be lifelong. You just have to reach a stage where you can function enough to carry on the activities of daily living and work.

If everything is taken from you, you still have your identity. Your identity is who you are. You must depend on yourself. You did it before. You must start building again. Only then will life change! Sometimes circumstances control you completely, but then you are given an opportunity to be in charge again. Whether you grab this opportunity depends on you. You will miss the opportunity if you are looking to others to give you what you want, if you are lost in brooding over your past, or if you are busy feeling sorry for yourself.

You can be miserable and depressed, or you can be calm and determined. Just think about the following: in case of divorce, would your children go to someone who is crying and poor, or someone who is successful and happy?

Do not cause your downfall.

Do not develop addictions.

Do not make impulsive decisions (resign, walk out).

Do not make emotional decisions to please others. Do not take up a job that you do not want. Do not go to work in a place where you will not be happy. Do not go to work in an unknown place unless you have the means to return.

Your Mantra is: "Just for one year, I will support myself and strive to become calm and confident.

Control your situation before it controls you!

Value time. There must be a time limit to lying around crying! Two months should do it. Stop your anti-depressants and anti-anxiety medications with the help of your doctor. Do not waste time or your life feeling sorry for yourself.

> Soon years will pass by, and you will be old, and you will deeply regret the time you wasted.

Is this what you want?

Value work. The routine of work soothes and heals you. You have a schedule in your life, and this is healthy and healing. Work gives you money and independence. Work gives you self-worth and self-respect. You get distracted by work. You form friends at work, and the loneliness is alleviated.

Value money. Do you want to beg others for money to support you?

Value yourself. You deserve better. You are going to use work to become independent and stronger.

> If you have no self-value, you will act as an enemy against your welfare. You will destroy yourself. Or you may kill the person causing you pain and spend the rest of your life in jail.

Energy Begets Energy.

Value your energy. You must get up and move. By lying around and crying, day after day, week after week, you will get weaker and add to your problems. When you move, you increase your energy. Your muscles pull on your bones and make them thicker. Your digestion is better. Your muscles become bulky. Your heart beats stronger to cope up with the movement. As your metabolism improves, more energy is produced.

But there is only so much energy you can make in a day. You can either use it to heal or to work. So, in the first few weeks, and on the days that you are overwhelmed, take time off.

Value your life. Do not compound your problems. Do not add poverty to your woes. Do not add ill health to your woes. Protect your mental health. Take time to relax. Do not jump into any new involvements for a year.

Focus on the present. Do not look back.

You develop willpower by forcing yourself to focus on the present instead of brooding over your past. Learn from the animals. They do not waste their energy by brooding over the past and so can enjoy the present.

This is your chance to grow up.

Make your own decisions. Depend on yourself to get what you want. Take charge of your life. Accept what you cannot get. Have goals with time limits. Remove any dependency. Find your self-respect. Develop your emotional boundary.

Be Wary of Your Emotions.

Decide by your mind, not by your emotions.

In bad times, our emotions are our worse enemy. They will tell us to stay home, live on our savings, cheat, steal, murder, or commit suicide. Do not listen to them.

Take charge of your mood.

If you act cheerfully, you will start becoming cheerful. Set your mental thermostat every morning to be cheerful, to be peaceful, to be grateful, and to be strong. You need gratitude to develop.

Give your mind a break.

Make time for some recreation daily. As a wise man pointed out, if you lift a weight, your arm gets tired after a while. You can no longer carry the burden. If you let your arm rest, it can again carry the burden. In the same way, if you rest your mind daily with non-chemical recreation, you can carry your burden of work and life. This can be with walks, pets, friends, shows, and so on.

Do not feel sorry for yourself, and do not ask others to feel sorry for you.

By feeling sorry for yourself, you destroy your zest for life.

Review the situation every three months for one year. Are you on the road to the strength and energy that you had before the tragedy happened? If not, what can you do to better yourself?

Acceptance

Acceptance always makes one stronger. "In acceptance lies peace." Accept the current situation. Accept that you are currently alone. Both may be temporary.

Let go of those who want to go. These may be your children, and this may be a temporary phase in your life.

Let go of the people who have hurt you and stole your happiness.

Learn from the animals. They go forward with all their pain, even when their young ones are taken away from them. Life is to go forward, no matter what happens.

Your reaction in bad times

Remember that bad times do not come in the shape you want

You can observe how people handle difficult times differently. One falls, then picks himself and faces life with determination. He has a reason to live, if only for the sake of his Maker. He has been taught to value himself, his work, and money. He has also been taught that life will come with good times and bad, and he must handle both.

The other one falls apart and becomes suicidal. He does not care that he has children to take care of or elderly parents to support. He is not setting the right example for his children. He does not value himself, his work, or his strength! He does not see work as a type of healing.

The difference in sexes

The situation is markedly different between a man and a woman. It is also different between a woman who has been taught to value herself and one who has not.

The Man

The man has it in his blood to keep working, no matter what is happening in his personal life. He thinks with his mind. He knows that no one else will support him, so he does not compound his woes. He values himself, his work, and his money.

As long as you value work and money, you should be able to survive.

The Woman

A. If a woman has self-value, and she suffers from abuse or a betrayal of trust.

She will say, "This is terrible. I do not deserve this. I deserve better."

Her self-respect and her self-protection will take over. She understands that she cannot control the other person's actions.

But she can certainly control the damage and repetition of abuse.

She takes the initiative and depends on herself to change the situation rather than wait for her relatives to do so. She will leave the terrible situation, but not on impulse. Being intelligent, she will plan her move.

Wise persons do not make emotional decisions.

They think over the pros and cons of their decisions before acting. So, the abused should decide where and when she will move. She should look for a job to support herself. She should make her new home and then fight her battles. She must get the self-confidence to do so.

She has shown that she values herself, work, and money.

B. If a woman has no self-value and has been taught to be "noble and self-sacrificing."

This woman has not been taught to value herself, work, or money! She has been abused. She has no self-respect and no identity of herself. She is emotionally dependent.

Her self-worth only comes from pleasing others or from her children being with her. When she has been betrayed or reached the limit of abuse, or if she has lost her children through death, divorce, or if they have rejected her, she will be paralyzed by grief and fall apart. She will lose her health.

She will not go to work because she is overcome by her sorrow. She will not care that she is becoming destitute. She will add ill health and poverty to her problems. She may become suicidal. She cannot hear words of advice and encouragement others offer her. Ultimately, she will destroy herself.

It does not occur to her that if her home is better and full of laughter, the children will want to come to her. She does not think that she should live in case her husband starts abusing the children, remarries, or drops dead.

If we handle our current situation with courage, we will come out much stronger and wiser.

When Should You Teach "A Protocol for Bad Times?"

This should be taught in advance *before* the bad times happen, preferably by the age of twelve.

First, the child needs to learn this to advance his development.

Second, you cannot teach this *later* to a person who now thinks that he knows everything.

Third, this cannot be taught during bad times. When one is involved in a situation, one cannot process new ideas.

However, one will fall back on what one already knows.

Fourth, intense emotions, whether sorrow, emotional pain, shock, anger, hatred, or depression, cover one like a thick blanket. Suggestions simply cannot penetrate.

If you value work, if you value money, if you value yourself and your self-respect, if you know that you cannot control the actions of others, if you can let go, if you understand that you have to face misfortunes at some point in your life, if you know that you have come on this earth for your development, you will be able to come out of this intact!

The questions you must ask are, "How can I protect myself, and what can I learn from this?"

PART EIGHT: WORKING WITH ABUSERS AND THE ABUSED

CHAPTER 30: WORK ETHICS OF ABUSED PEOPLE

It is necessary to teach proper "work behavior" to your children or students if you want them to be productive and society to prosper. Work behavior must be taught from middle school.

> It is especially critical to teach work behavior, besides work skills, to those who have been abused if you want them to survive.

A child who is abused cannot absorb the work ethics of her parents, as all her energy has gone into trying to survive, protecting her loved ones, and keeping her sanity.

She could have been treated with so much contempt that she may have lost all her self-confidence.

She could have been treated with so much anger that she has become fearful.

She may have only learned to be self-sacrificing, which, in her case, can become self-destructive.

In an abused atmosphere, she may not have been allowed to think and make decisions for herself.

In a home that is a battlefield, there may be no role model for her to follow.

She does not know how to treat her juniors or customers. She only knows to abuse or be abused.

Such a child will get destroyed unless she is taught to value herself, work, and money as well as correct work behavior.

Where can she be taught this before she applies for a job? If her work behavior is lacking, she will lose her job. This will further increase her inferiority complex.

She must be told that "work behavior" exists as an entity. She must ask her friends. She should read self-help books. She can be offered this book, as well as the book on abuse, by the author, titled, "Are you abused or an abuser?"

When an abused person enters the workforce, she must *not* be given employment in positions where she deals with people.

Social services should let the employer know that she should not be given a job dealing with customers because of certain circumstances. There is no need to inform the employer that she has been abused because then he may abuse her. She should have a position where she can carry on work alone, such as in computers, bookkeeping, factories, and putting items on shelves or mathematical transections. She must not be given a job entailing responsibilities and involving decisions. This can change once she starts coming out of her fear.

After marriage

When an abused woman marries a man who loves her, she may think that she has finally found someone who values her. It is a haven after all the abuse that she has endured. Unfortunately, the workplace is unknown to her.

Therefore, she will value her home high over her work. This thinking is dangerous!

The man may have had other reasons to marry her. He may want her paycheck. The man may now pick up her vibrations of being abused and start abusing her. So now she will further lose her self-confidence, besides her money. As long as she is earning money, he will not do so, but what happens if she decides to stay home to raise the children? She is no longer bringing in a paycheck. He will start abusing her. What happens if he is unfaithful and leaves her? What happens if he dies?

It is paramount that an abused woman holds a job to validate herself and that she gives her work and family equal importance.

She must not value one over the other.

What does it mean to validate herself? It means that she matters, what she does matters, and she needs to support herself. She must not add poverty to her stress. She must learn to value her work, and she must learn work behavior

It is critical that she not turn over all her money to her spouse but keep half for herself.

As long as she has some money, the abuser will treat her well.

Is she capable of working?

If, besides her husband, she is also abused by her parents and siblings, then it will be quite difficult for her to work.

How can she work when she is overcome with emotional pain and abandonment by the very people, she considered her own and trusted for security? How can she focus on giving excellence when she is suicidal? If her children have been taken away from her in a divorce, she may be going crazy with worry!

Period of recovery

She needs to take some months off and be in a "sheltered cocoon." She is not capable of working. But after a few months, she cannot just lie passively crying.

Then, she must use the time to actively heal herself by getting help.

She has to bring her shattered self together and re-establish her identity. She has to find a "why to live" in order to find a "how to live."

She must stay alive in case her spouse dies and her children need her. She must do better than her spouse so that her children come back to her. If she has no children, she should know that she has been sent to this earth for her personal development. What is happening to her may be the very scenario needed for her to have courage, grow up, and become independent. She must develop the faith that there is something better around the corner.

CHAPTER 31: SHOULD YOU HIRE AN ABUSER?

A person who is abusive at home, immoral, addictive, or breaks the law, cannot be kept at work. This is because, at all times, we must protect our society. All companies have a responsibility to do so. So do all government jobs since it is the responsibility of the government to protect society.

> Second, the threat of losing a job is one of the strongest deterrents to prevent abuse.

Third, the character flows into work. An abuser may appear submissive at work, but greed, selfishness, cruelty, arrogance, anger, and non-caring cannot be left outside the business doors. They do creep in.

Fourth, it promotes the message that wrong behavior does not prevent you from going on to earning a living that you are used to.

> It means that as a company or an institution, we condone a wrong behavior

Fifth, the company's reputation is at stake. The company cannot afford to be known for keeping abusers. We must show that such behavior will not be tolerated.

Once a spouse, doctor, police, or others report to the employer that an employee is abusive at home, the employer must sit down with an employee. He must warn him that his personal life does affect his ability to keep a job. He must warn him that this information will now go into his file.

He should also warn him that half his salary will be put in his spouse's name if his behavior is repeated. Furthermore, after his third offense against moral behavior, the employee will be fired. All this must be made legal to protect our society.

An employer plays an essential role in preventing abuse in the family and society.

CHAPTER 32: SHOULD AN ABUSED PERSON BE SELF-EMPLOYED?

A private business requires tremendous energy, work, time, focus, planning, and dedication. A business will not run by itself. It also means that you need specific goals with time limits.

Business needs all your time and focus.

You cannot do this if you are battling with personal turmoil, sorrow, or loss. You will use up your time and energy when you are busy brooding over your loss or how you were treated by others in the past, or currently by people at home.

Understand that you create only so much energy daily.

When you are abused, all your energy is being consumed in handling the abuse, keeping your sanity, and fighting your depression. Where is the energy left to go into the business?

When your mind is distracted in so many directions, where is the focus for your business?

If you are deciding whether to live or die, how can the business hold any importance for you?

Also, if you are battling with personal turmoil or sorrow, the customer can sense your aura.

The customer will be more attracted to one who is happy, vibrant, and at peace. Would you not be so?

Running a business is not for one who is feeling sorry for oneself.

Feeling sorry for yourself always removes your zest for life.

You should not ask others to feel sorry for you, because that is manipulation.

If you have no self-confidence, you will not succeed.

(You can learn about regaining your self - confidence in the author's book on development).

If you have no goals with time limits, if you have no passion for succeeding, and no enthusiasm to overcome obstacles, you will not succeed.

An employer has a variety of situations that need his constant attention at work. In business, you do not just carry out work duties. You are planning, competing, dealing with losses, finances, etc. If you do not attend to them, you cannot pay yourself and your employees.

A person who has been abused as a child can work for others, but he should never start a business for himself

This is because of the following.

He is scared to death.

He has an inferiority complex.

He has repeatedly been told that he is no good.

He has no self-confidence.

He is drowning in pain.

He has not been taught "work behavior."

He has no one to emulate.

He does not know the skills to be an employer.

He has no interpersonal skills.

He is plagued by depression, and so has no joy in his work.

He has no pride in his work, no burning desire to succeed, and no drive to offer excellence.

If the abused is a woman, the people she turns to for help sense that she is abused, or feels inferior, and will take advantage of her.

Financially

The purpose of your business is to make money,
But the abused cannot collect the payments owed to him.

Firstly, he is depressed, so he does not have the incentive.

Secondly, he was brainwashed to take care of others and not worry about himself. So, he is not interested.

Thirdly, he has no financial skills. He does not know how to collect payment for the services he offers.

Fourthly, he may have been taught that "money is dirty" so he is reluctant to go after it.

Fifthly, he does not value himself, so he does not go after what he deserves.

When you work for someone else

When you work for someone else, you get a paycheck every two weeks. You do not have to worry about where it will come from, nor do you have to make efforts to collect it.

When you work for someone, you can put all your focus into just one thing, that is doing what you are told to do.

After five pm, you no longer have to think about the business.

The survival of the company does not depend on you.

So, you have removed these anxieties.

You can focus on taking care of your recovery.

One who is abused, should work for others until:

He has let go of abusive people.

He has overcome his loss.

He has got his self-confidence.

He has overcome his depression.

He has healed from within and got his inner strength.

He has found a reason to live.

PART NINE: DO YOU WANT TO RUN YOUR BUSINESS?

CHAPTER 33: THE EMPLOYER

At work, you must hire the best person possible and one who has experience.

The success of your business depends on this. Interview your prospective employees with great care and be prepared to spend the extra money needed. Go by their experience and their recommendations. Never hire a beginner if your company is also starting up or floundering. Never hire a beginner if you do not have someone senior to guide him.

> Start small, grow a business, and then move to a larger space.

We can work well for others, but we may not know how to start a business. We may buy a huge property which then sits vacant for years.

> Always spend a year in apprenticeship before you open your practice.

You know nothing about the administration aspect or how to handle your clients.

> One must actively promote one's business.

It is not enough to go to your store and wait passively for a customer to walk in and attend to him. You have to go out and make yourself known by attending events, joining local associations, and meeting others.

> Work very hard the first five years and put in long hours until your company takes off.

Having your own business is vastly different from working for someone else. Your work does not finish at five pm.

> Work without enthusiasm, self-discipline and planning cannot succeed.

You must have the enthusiasm for your business, the passionate desire for it to succeed. When you work for yourself, you must work harder and show more discipline than when you work for others. You must plan and oversee every detail, every day, until the business takes off. You must be present all day. See the next chapter for details. Besides this, remember that "it is not the time you put in the work, but the work you put in the time."

> Working hard means nothing if you are not achieving anything.

This is where the time limit comes in. Do not give more than six months to your project if you are not making progress. Sometimes luck plays a vital role.

> Do not go into private business if you are not willing to give your time and energy.

Private business requires tremendous energy, focus, dedication and planning. If you are not willing to put in the time, you will not succeed.

> A business will not run by itself.

Never go into business if you have to spend energy elsewhere (court battles, divorce, family issues, and so on). In business, you must be present in the office, and you must be an active participant, not passive.

How are you feeling?

Never go into business if you have an inferiority complex or are depressed. Your feelings, your depression, fears, inferiority complex, the pain from your personal life, as well as your non-caring about the business, are ninety-nine percent reflected in your face and attitude. This can have terrible consequences on your business. It is better to develop calm and enthusiasm before you start a business

Your face reveals your inner you.

If you are depressed or unsure, the customer can sense it. Would he not rather go to an owner who is cheerful, confident, energetic, enthusiastic, pleasant, and patient? Your store is your personality. Your employees, too, will be affected by your approach to your business. If you are passionate about your store, they will be too.

An employer works harder than his employees. He wears many hats

He works nights and weekends. He takes more risks than his employees. He is responsible for his company's infrastructure and ensures it runs smoothly. This includes overseeing bank loans, managing supplies, supervising workers, writing job descriptions, handling the payroll, creating or approving advertisements, and the timing of when different projects are run, and jobs are completed. He has to attract customers and retain them. He must deal with difficult people, keep up with local laws, and compete with competitors. He must track and collect the money owed to him.

There are three types of workers:

1. One who wants to cheat the customer,

2. One who does not take work seriously, does a slipshod job, takes his pay, and leaves, and

3. One who offers excellence. But it is not enough to offer excellence. You must help the customer. Be cheerful and interested in the customer's needs.

Get back to the customer in a timely manner.

Keep your word to the customer and never lie to him. To say, "I told you, etc.," to a customer, when you did not, tells him that you cannot be trusted.

Do not show your anger to a customer. Would you like to be treated with anger?

Treat the customer with respect.

Do not act too familiar with a customer. You should act professionally and not ask prying questions about the family or work etc.

Your goal is to keep the customer. Make him happy that he chose you and gain his trust. It should not happen that when the work is good, you take all the credit, but when your work is bad, you accuse the customer, "You are looking for defects. I do not want to work with you again. I do not want your money."

These are signs of a person with an inferiority complex. A person who has no inferiority complex would say, "I am sorry that you do not like it. What can I do to make you like it? Let me see if I can afford it. If I am wrong, I will swallow the expenses."

CHAPTER 34: WHAT DO YOU NEED TO SUCCEED?

1. If you do not value yourself, work, and money, how can you succeed?

2. If you cannot get along with people, customers, and employees, how can you succeed? You need a social circle.

3. Without goals and deadlines, you should not even begin this venture. You must value time and have goals with time limits of not more than two years.

4. You need capital to survive the initial year or two.

5. You need to be willing to work extremely hard.

6. You need to have enthusiasm, self-discipline and planning. "Failing to plan is planning to fail." See further down in this chapter.

7. You must not be afraid of money.

The whole aim here is to make a profit. Do not blindly trust others to take care of your money. How many entertainers have gone bankrupt because they trusted other people to be honest and manage their money?

8. You must have a completely organized system

Have your files organized. Organize your routines on coming in and on leaving. Know when to take care of the work pending from the previous day and organize the priority of the work of today. Set the time for phone calls and the time to work uninterrupted. Have the list of work to be done tomorrow. Have a day for ordering supplies and plan how garbage will be removed. Have a backup plan if your employee does not show up.

And organize your payment system from:

> from the time the customer came in to:
>
> how the bill is paid or sent out,
>
> how to track if and when the bill was paid,
>
> the time given for it to be paid,
>
> what to do when it is not paid

and to weekly reconcile your bills with receipts and see if you are in the red or black.

9. Besides all this, there is an element of *luck* that may be unfavorable.

10. *You must know when to quit.*

Attitude

> You will not succeed if you think that people should help you because they feel sorry for you.

A positive attitude is everything!

> You need enthusiasm and a burning desire to succeed. You must have self-confidence, cheerfulness and dedication to work.

You should remove anyone in your personal life who causes you to lose these qualities. You are being given a chance to show us what you are capable of.

Go for it!

Self-discipline

Since you have no boss, you must demand from yourself the very things that your boss would have demanded from you. Since you have no one to tell you what to do, it is critical that you become your own boss.

Self-discipline is critical.

It means you cannot procrastinate.

It means you must not work in fits and starts.

You cannot allow your personal life to affect your work.

You must wake up at a set time and be at the workplace at a fixed time every day.

You must oversee every detail. All things needing your attention must be attended to.

Work must be finished daily as far as possible.

All calls should be returned. Everything should be organized, and no time wasted looking for things.

Supplies must be ordered at a set time, besides when needed.

Planning

You must plan for your business to succeed. You must plan:

the *financial aspect.*

the *description of the business*, what you will offer, how you will offer it, the hours of work and your availability.

the *advertising,* the way to acquire customers and become known.

the way to handle *competition,* to have competitive pricing, and

the *management* of employees. This management includes planning the work duties for the employees, their payroll and benefits, and handling any employee problems, including absenteeism.0

Decision-making

Always think carefully about all aspects of your problem before you come to a decision

Never make decisions on an impulse!

You do not always have to make your decision on the spot. Give yourself twenty-four hours to decide. Remember, there is no perfect decision. There is only the best decision in the given circumstances. Check your "benefits versus risk" ratio and see if you can handle the worst that can happen from your decision.

You do not have to give a reason for your decisions unless it helps to do so. Hear the suggestions and complaints from others. Consider these but make your own decision.

Never make a decision in anger!

Be Calm.

Try to stay calm throughout the day. Do not allow others to irritate you.

A calm employer gets more out of his employees than a volatile one.

When your brain gets tired or under a lot of pressure, take some time off for recreation. It will recharge your battery.

CHAPTER 35: MANAGING YOUR STAFF

Work does not give you the permission to hit an employee, throw things at him, physically punish him, privately demean him or publicly humiliate him. However, his actions may have to be made public in order to protect the company. This applies to both sexes. You are not allowed to make sexual advances or have a sexual atmosphere that makes him or her uncomfortable.

There must be no intimidation at work, nor should you expect blind obedience. These can cause terrible mistakes.

At least a month of leave for death must be given. It is cruelty to give only a couple of weeks. The human milestones cannot be ignored.

Leave must be given for the first year after a childbirth. Our children are our next generation, and their welfare must supersede those of others.

Since the small employer cannot survive this, he must be allowed to give benefits for a period per his profits based on his quarterly tax returns. He must also be allowed to hire temporarily from an employment pool. And the government must add to, or replace, the funeral and childbirth wages for those affected.

This will not apply to companies with over one hundred employees as they can afford to do this.

Your Behavior.

Keep your customers happy and keep your staff happy.

Have self-discipline yourself. Be at work at a fixed time every morning. Make a schedule and stick to it.

Keep your distance. Do not share your private life, fears, or pain with your employees. You are their boss, not their friend.

Dress properly.

Be organized and conscientious.

Show enthusiasm for your work. Your enthusiasm is critical.

Have humility

You should be able to do the same work that your workers do. Do not be afraid to get your hands dirty.

Who Do You Hire?

Having a good employee means winning half the battle.

Your employee is important for your business. Spend the time and effort in looking for a good employee.

Whom you hire has to be a carefully thought-out decision. It will determine whether you have pain or relief, and whether you will have success or failure. Therefore, it is not a decision to be taken lightly. You want to hire a person for many years, and you want to take your time to choose someone. Steve Jobs used to interview applicants for twelve hours and then bring back the candidate the next day.

Do not hire a family member.

It will create jealousy and resentment. It is
sometimes impossible to fire family members if they
perform poorly. You will always ruin relationships since
your relatives do not meet your expectations and vice versa.
They want special favors. The balance in relationships is
lost.

Your business needs enthusiasm.

> Do not hire someone who is going through
> emotional turmoil or is depressed.

Do not hire out of charity.

It is far better to donate to a charity. Your business
cannot survive without capable employees.

Take your time to find the best candidate for the
position. Use a reliable temporary agency until then. Make
sure that you have time to study the candidate at work, so
offer him a trial period.

Get references.

Get feedback from the candidate's prior boss, not a
colleague. Make sure it is someone who checks and
supervises his work. Did the candidate follow instructions?
Did he focus? Was he on time? Did he rush out the door
without finishing his duties? How did he act when he is
corrected? Did he roll his eyes to show that he did not
agree? Was he argumentative? Was he organized? Did he
have a list of things to do, that others could finish if he did
not show up? How did he treat his customers and
colleagues? See if he stayed at least a year in his previous
positions. See if he has worked recently. See if he has skills
in the fields you need.

Is the applicant using this as a stepping-stone in his career? Does he need the job or the skills of your office? If he has worked in a big office, he might look down upon your office as too small. And even after all this work, you may still not get the right candidate!

How Do You Treat Your Staff?

Respect them. Praise them at times.

Do not show favoritism. Treat everyone fairly.

Keep your word to your employees. Your employees should be able to trust that you will be fair, impartial, and considerate. Protect your employees as far as possible. Do not discuss with them your plans for the termination of other employees.

Have a hiring protocol and a firing protocol.

Sometimes an employee is not capable of doing the work that you had hired him for. He is just not suitable for it but may flourish in something else.

You cannot put a square peg in a round hole!

Sometimes an employee cannot perform the work because he is terrified. It may be a mathematical work or a software program. If you remove him from that type of work, he may, after some time, be curious enough (or have learned enough) to see if he can do it. Let him do this without letting him know that you are watching him.

Do not keep a person who disrespects you, will not follow your orders, or cannot focus on his job.

Since their work depends on your work, you must work hard. Remember that it is your dedication and enthusiasm that will make your juniors work better, rather than their fear of you.

Let your employees do the details, so you are free to plan new projects.

Be clear.

Your employees must know what you expect from them. Once you make rules, enforce them. Work descriptions must be clear. Be clear about hours and duties. Give them a reasonable deadline and *prioritize* your work details for them. Check their work. Ask for their input, which you may or may not follow. They do not always have to know a reason for your decision. There must be clarity of instructions, but there must be some flexibility depending on the circumstances.

Make sure the workload is fairly distributed. Sometimes this gets forgotten in the hectic pace, especially if you are facing tight deadlines. Go over the work given to them weekly to prevent this.

An employer must give an hour for lunch to his workers. He must change jobs involving manual repetition of the same muscles every hour. He must give laborers half-hour breaks between starting time and lunchtime and between lunch and closing time. He cannot deny the right of a worker to use the bathroom when needed.

What do you do about an excellent worker who is demeaning and insulting other workers? He has become a toxic employee. You cannot have a divided office. This worker must be fired.

How Do You Scold Your Employee?

Read the chapter on "do-nots in scolding" in this book.

Respond to the complaints from the colleagues of your employee and act. Otherwise, the morale will go down.

Do not scold your employees when you first walk in.

Do not call them at home to scold them unless it is to prevent something from happening. Neither should you scold anyone in your family when you first walk in. Greet them pleasantly.

> Show your temper only to the degree that is necessary and calm down immediately.

Do not lose your temper. Do not shout. Keep an even voice. Say, "This is unacceptable. This is not how I want things to run." Become calm immediately. *Let him "save face."* Simply state what you will and will not tolerate. Your aim is not to tell the employees that they are bad.

> Your only goal is to make sure that this problem does not reoccur.

Do not insult your workers. Treat them as you would want to be treated if you were in their shoes.

Do not let him be embarrassed or humiliated in front of his family.

Do not scold him in front of his colleague, a patient, a customer, or a visitor.

Stick to the action, not the person.

Expect your employees to make a mistake occasionally.

How Do You Fire Your Employee?

If your employee resigns, accept it gracefully.

Have a protocol for firing and follow it. Give two warnings before considering termination. At the second warning, provide a performance improvement plan. Have him sign it. If he refuses to sign it, note that. Fire him at the third repetition of the same behavior.

There are times when you cannot wait for this type of protocol, for example, if the employee is disrespectful or refuses to follow your instructions. Then you must fire him immediately.

Before you fire him, put down your thoughts on paper to clarify why you are firing him. You can give him this letter. Do not raise your voice. Do not fight with him. Calmly say, "I regret that I have to let you go." Do not apologize or get into an argument. Do not help him to look for another job. There will be no recommendation letter.

Do not fire him in front of his colleagues. Try to do it when others are not there or bring him to your office at the end of the day or early morning. Try not to do it before a holiday unless you have reached the limit of your tolerance.

Do not allow him to go about the office and speak to his colleagues. They are upset and embarrassed. Instead, stay while he collects his belongings and returns the office keys. Stay until he has left. Make sure that an administrator resets any passwords he needs to log in remotely.

CHAPTER 36: THE "DO-NOTS" FOR THE EMPLOYER

Do not make your employees do what they cannot do well.

Do not waste your time trying to get an unorganized employee to become organized.

Do not do your employee's work for him. If you cannot trust him to do his job well, do not give him the job in the first place.

Know that employees will make some mistakes. But do not allow them to repeat a mistake more than twice.

Do not blindly trust your employees. Have a system of checks and counterchecks.

Do not take favors from employees.

Do not mix the professional jobs of your employees with personal jobs for yourself.

Do not keep an employee if you are having friction with him.

Do not keep a bad employee. It is better to fire a bad employee than to limp along with him and ruin your business. Fire him quickly before he can influence others or before he causes others to lose morale.

Do not demoralize your employee by giving him more work than he can handle. Listen to him when he says that he is overloaded. That does not mean that he is not a good worker.

Do not make him work seven days a week. This is immoral. Understand that an employee has a private life. Do not come in late and start a meeting when it is his time to leave (unless it is an unavoidable emergency.

Do not make an employee feel stupid for asking questions. He needs some time to understand his job, during which he must be allowed to ask questions, forgiven for making mistakes, and guided. During this time, it is his supervisor who is responsible for his actions.

CHAPTER 37: THE "DO'S" FOR THE EMPLOYER

Organize yourself when you come in.

Do not discuss things with the staff immediately.

Settle down first. Get your supplies for the day: pad, pen, turn on your computer, check critical information, etc.

Ask if there is anything urgent that must be handled immediately.

Check your messages. Give your replies.

Do not keep the staff waiting. See that the staff have instructions to carry on their work while you are working, then finish your "personal" list.

Prioritize your personal list.

You have a calendar and a notebook on your computer.

Check your calendar for meetings for the day.

Attend to what is marked urgent.

Check your mail.

Return calls.

Attend meetings.

Check what supplies are needed.

See what repairs must be scheduled.

See which employee needs to take off and rearrange the schedule accordingly.

See what money has come in.

Fill the needed forms.

Sign your reports.

Do your dictation.

Then do your "regular work." Of course, in between all this, you will be getting phone calls that you must answer.

Recall your staff after one hour unless there is an issue that must be decided urgently. Go over the work they did. See what questions they have and what they need.

Refuse to let the staff walk in every time that they think of something.

This includes the work they have completed. Having the staff walking in and out of your office becomes distracting for you. Ask them to make a list unless it is urgent. Ask them, "Does this have to be decided upon right now?"

Designate timelines and days as far as possible.
When are your reports sent out?
When do you order supplies?
When do the bills go out?
When are the meetings with the staff? And so on.
Having a routine will make it easier to remember when specific tasks are to be completed for you and your employees.

CHAPTER 38: HANDLE THE INTERPERSONAL PROBLEMS OF EMPLOYEES

Do not give general statements

A. Do not say, "You are not ready for this position." Explain why.

B. Do not say, "You can rise above this." Explain how. Be specific and address each problem and show a better way. You can tell an employee, "Instead of your saying, "Why is everyone picking on me?" you should have been willing to apologize if you were wrong or made it inconvenient for everyone."

C. Do not say, "You three, figure out how to handle each other." If they could have, they would not have come to you.

If the employees come to the employer because they have a problem with one another, understand that they may genuinely not know how to handle it, or they want you to do the work of making them get along with each other. This cannot be allowed too often as they must find a way to get along.

Understand the following:

One of your employees may be angry, disrespectful, and insulting.

He may be one who thinks he knows everything and so is incapable of learning.

He may be irresponsible and shirking his work.

He may not have been taught at home how to get along with others. He does not have the consideration, tact, and self-control required for this.

He may be in a family where one is an abuser and one abused, and everyone is fighting for control.

He may be spoiled at home or may have never been told "no."

He may have no work ethics

In such a situation, you cannot make this person grow up. *That is not your job.* You have to let such a person go after two warnings.

If an employee comes to you and says that he cannot get along with another, you need clarification.

First, say:

"Write down the problem and send it to me, and I will get back to you in one week."

This does a few things.

You have time to:

calmly review the complaint without their emotional selves being present,

think about your response and come up with suggestions,

and, if needed, get advice.

When they write down what is bothering them:

They become more thoughtful.

They can clarify the problem in their head and see their behavior more clearly.

They can see the response they want.

They have a "cooling off" period so that they will listen more rationally to you without the heat of the battle; and

They have a chance of reviewing what they said and modifying it.

Second

Tell your employee that when they write this, they must address the following points:

Did you take this personally as an attack on yourself?

Did you become defensive and try to defend yourself?

Did you counterattack?

Were you able to acknowledge that you caused an inconvenience to another? Were you considerate?

Were you able to acknowledge that you were wrong?

Did you defuse the situation by apologizing quickly?

Did you offer a quick response to the problem requested, or did you spend time grumbling about how many times you have addressed this before?

Say to your employee, "If you did offer the solution to your colleague before, please give me this solution in writing so that I can see if you were clear in your advice."

Third

If the employee says that he wants to discuss an unrelated problem, say, "We will not add another complaint with this one. We will focus on this alone today."

Fourth,

If the employee says, "I do not feel that I am being treated fairly or this is not what I came to this company for," respond by saying, "We will discuss this another time, or you can go to Human Resources for this. Today we will stay focused on the original problem."

Close the meeting quickly. Say, "You can leave now. I have other work to do."

CHAPTER 39: CRITERIA FOR FIRING

Whom you hire, how you scold, and when to fire is knowledge critical for your company.

It is interesting how an abused employer will think. He questions himself often with thoughts like the following:

"If I behave better, will she behave better?"

"Am I scared that people would think that I am not a good employer?"

"Do I want to go through the trouble of finding another employee?"

(Yes. It is worth the peace and smooth functioning of the office).

"Did I give enough time for her to better herself in this office?"

(One day to two weeks is enough).

"Did I give enough chances?"

(Two chances are enough).

"Did I talk to her about her behavior? Did she continue to repeat it?"

Hire slowly but fire fast.

Two things must be understood.

You cannot change the employee by talking to her long enough or keeping her long enough.

She is to be taken at face value for who she is and be dealt with accordingly. Second,

A bad employee will influence others to be bad.

Fire for the following.

Is she competent?

Is she disrespectful and arrogant? Does she treat you, her colleagues, or the customers with contempt?

Is she dishonest or stealing?

Is she depressed or angry?

Can she focus, or is she distracted?

Does she follow your instructions or disobey or neglect them?

Does she have to be told twice or more? *Does she make the same mistake repeatedly?*

If she is not following your instructions, why are you keeping her?

Does she think when she acts, or does she follow instructions blindly?

Does she want to change the office to her way at once or after some time?

Does she waste office material?

Does she protect the office?

Can she handle criticism? Does she fight back or refuse to apologize?

Is she dependable and responsible?

Does she repeatedly do what bothers you?

Is she punctual?

Does she keep taking time off?

Does she stay the time?

Does she run out at the clock, or does she get the office ready for the next day before she leaves?

Does she treat the customers nicely?

Does she get along with her colleagues?

Does she refuse to help them?

Does she want them to help her most of the time?

Is she neat and organized?

Does she have to be reminded of her work because she will not write it down?

Does she return calls the next day?

Does she finish the work of the week, that week, and urgent work that day?

Does she have files and papers prepared for the next day?

Does she always have an excuse as to why she did not do the work?

Does she insist that she has a right to forget but does not want the boss to forget to give her a paycheck?

Is she nice to the boss but arrogant to her workers or vice versa?

Does she hide behind the sentence, "I do not know why I did that?" This shows a complete lack of responsibility and focus.

Is she in denial? "I do my work! I pull my load."

Is she stealing your customers for herself?

PART TEN: TEACH WORK BEHAVIOR TO OUR NEXT GENERATION.

CHAPTER 40: LET US TEACH OUR CHILDREN

Learning of appropriate "work behavior" cannot be left to chance. The parents must offer their sons and daughters the same skills and education, including education about behavior at work.

Knowing the proper work behavior is the difference between:

> being abused, or being free from abuse,
>
> feeling worthless, or having self-worth,
>
> dependency or independence,
>
> happiness or sadness,
>
> having an inferiority complex or having confidence,
>
> poverty, or self-sustenance,
>
> crime or law-abiding behavior and
>
> peace or terror.

Generations are affected.

The effects of wrong work behavior are not restricted to just one person but are felt in the generations after him because each succeeding generation learns the same misfit behavior. Just consider the loss of human potential! Every society is affected by its workforce and poverty. These, in turn, depend on the capability of the worker.

Work behavior is a critical life skill that cannot be left to chance, on the personality of one's family or how one was treated by the world.

Work behavior must be taught at school in an age-appropriate, systematic way from six years of age.

Any teacher will tell you the following:

> A child with the qualities of self-value, self-worth, self-respect, self-confidence, self-control, and self-discipline), who can also delay gratification and handle frustration without violence, does far better than others.

It is as if the parent has given him additional skills to handle the school and the world.

We start with *"VALUES"* and then proceed to the acronym R.E.A.C.T.

A. VALUES

The child must be given *self-value*, and therefore, *self-confidence*. He must be given *self-worth*.

The child must know that it is okay to make mistakes and that he will learn from them. Neither his mistakes nor his efforts should ever be laughed at by his parents.

The teacher, too, can stress his worth. A student knows when the teacher likes him, even though she is correcting him and stopping him from doing what he wants.

What is the difference between having self-value and being selfish?

> In selfishness, you *do* whatever your feelings tell you to do.
>
> In self-value, you fight against your feelings.

Only an abuser makes fun of his children!

If the parent makes all the decisions for the child, if the parent is over-protective, if a child cannot make a meal for himself or take care of his clothes, how can he have self-confidence?

The parent cannot be over-protective.

Only a *controlling* parent will not allow his child to choose what he wants to do in school. The child has to make decisions for himself and only stopped if he is in danger of hurting himself. He should not live in fear of being ridiculed and treated with consistent anger and contempt. He is not to be humiliated outside. He must not be made to feel helpless and his feelings unappreciated.

The child must not be made to follow orders blindly.

There should be no struggle for power between parents.

The parents must not contradict each other in front of the child.

The child must have a structured timetable at home.

He needs definite times to sleep, wake up, eat, and play so that he is not at the mercy of his feelings.

Frustration and Gratification

The child cannot always do whatever he wants, whenever he wants.

The child needs to handle frustration and delay his gratification, which ultimately gives him self-control, inner strength, and, therefore, self-value.

One example of delaying gratification is that he cannot eat the cookie or a toy that you bought in a store until he gets home. So many studies have shown that delaying gratification is vital for success in life, e.g., "the marshmallow test."

> And handling frustration is equally critical! The inner strength and inner peace obtained are outstanding.

The parents must show the child how to handle frustrations.

> But for this, the parent too must be able to delay his gratification and handle frustrations.

If the parent can only react by cursing, throwing objects, and breaking things whenever he does not get his way, then he is not fit to teach the child. It only shows that the parent is immature and has no self-control. Television and movies portray a very wrong way to handle frustrations and must be stopped from doing so.

The school must stress the following to the parents:

- The parents are to be parents. The child has enough friends. He needs parents who are mentors.
- The parents must never make fun of their child or his efforts.
- They must never treat him with contempt or consistent anger.
- **He is not on this earth to fulfill their dreams. He has his own dreams and talents to achieve.**
- They must not manipulate him with guilt.

- They should never speak badly about him to others or humiliate him in public.
- His punishment cannot be out of proportion to the misdeed.

He must have responsibilities for age-appropriate home chores.

This cannot be over-emphasized!

B. "R.E.A.C.T."

The child must be taught work behavior by the guidelines set in the acronym R.E.A.C.T

R stands for Relationships.

A child needs to be taught how to get along with adults as well as those of his age group.

It means not being selfish, not bullying, not making fun of another, not ostracizing another, handling frustrations, sharing, and working as a team.

It requires consideration, manners, and being fair. Caring for one another must be encouraged. Caring also develops when we take care of animals.

Any sign of cruelty must be immediately stopped.

E stands for Excellence.

The child is taught to do his best. He usually will, unless he is tired, ill, or not interested that day, in which case, do not force him.

The parent can teach him how to organize by letting him choose the previous night, his clothes for the next day.

He should put away the current game before he moves to the next one. He should finish what he starts, even if it is by the next day because of his shorter attention span.

A stands for Appearance.

The child is encouraged to be clean and neat. He should put his toys away in a basket or other place at night before retiring. His work should be neatly put away.

C stands for Character. It also stands for Cleanliness.

Cleanliness

Why should cleanliness be taught in a book on work? Who wants to walk into a dirty office?

His room should be clean within his capacity. You must teach him cleanliness not only in your home *but also in the environment outside his home.* If you do not care about the trash outside your house, your child, on growing up, will not care about the trash outside his shop.

He must not throw garbage anywhere except in a container. If he sees any garbage outside, he should pick it up and put it in a container; or put it in a bag and bring it home to dispose of it.

Pollution causes illness, and if you are ill, you cannot work. Personal development also means taking care of our planet and the animals in it and leave it clean for the next generation.

Why should he be neat?

When we are neat, we waste less time looking for things. We are more organized in our approach. There is more peace in neat surroundings than in a chaotic one.

Those who say "do not mess with my mess" are not every efficient people.

Character:

The child must be given the foundation of a good character.

One of the duties of every parent is to teach his child morals and ethics so that he has clarity of how to behave when he is faced with any situation in his life. One should also teach him modesty and decency, two words that have disappeared from our language, and yet both words lead to control over our emotions.

> When he reads stories of brave, honest, and noble people, you will have planted seeds of courage and morality.

When you allow youth to read books that are sexually exciting, you must understand that they will get addicted to sex. They become" sexaholics." They will damage their lives and those of others around them. You can see this with sexual harassment in the workplace.

> Never have sexual jokes with your children, nor watch sexual movies with them.

Anyone who calls sex "an appetite like other appetites "has his head buried in the sand.

No other appetite produces another human being, a baby whose life gets ruined and even destroyed. Just look at all the infanticides in our society. Look at all the young people who had to go to jail for killing their children. Listen to the pain of those who had to be adopted. What other human appetite does that?

> The best things that we can pass on to our children are our courage and morals.

T stands for time.

If the child wakes up at a fixed time every day, he develops a body clock and no longer has any difficulty doing so.

If he wakes up early enough, he has time to get ready, have breakfast, and play for a little while. He goes to school in a relaxed mood instead of running hungry after the bus.

Let him know that, in fifteen to thirty minutes, he will have to stop playing, go to bed or that the dinner will start.

> This reduces the anxiety that occurs if he does not know when he must stop his activity suddenly.

As he gets older, he learns to finish his projects in time or by a specific date. His activities for playing or sleeping are structured.

The work must be appropriate for the child's capability and not beyond it. The parents must never force their child to do any work when he is ill or tired.

A child must be allowed to grow up.

You must grow up in order to live on this earth fully. An adult remains childlike if he is not allowed to grow up.

This happens in two ways.

First, when a parent does not want to give up his power to make all the decisions for his adult child, he takes away the child's self-confidence. So, the child will remain childlike and dependent.

On the other hand, if the child is allowed to make all his decisions (right or wrong) from an early age and told that he is right, and the other adults around him are wrong, then his personal growth gets stunted.

He becomes a puppet run by his emotions and impulses since he has no control over himself.

Secondly, his learning has stopped. He thinks that he knows more than others. Since he has contempt for adults, he cannot learn from them.

He has not been taught self-control, control over frustration and anger, manners, or moral principles to guide him.

He will have pain in his life and bring pain to those he touches.

Both these factors lead to the development of a person who cannot do well in the workforce.

PART ELEVEN: DEVELOPMENT

CHAPTER 41: DEVELOPMENT

To know that, like your family life and spiritual life, work is an equally important aspect of your life and needs the same effort and time,

To separate your work from your personal life,

to take pride in financially sustaining yourself (even when your personal life is falling apart),

to look forward to going to work,

to get satisfaction from your work,

or to leave, if possible, when you do not like your job,

to offer excellence and to keep your word,

to help your customer,

to stay within the moral boundary,

to have goals with time limits,

to take no impulsive decisions at work, and

to never be attached to a place of work or occupation,

this is one aspect of development!

Conclusion

Work is the other equally important half of your life. It is important to value it.

It is a wise man who understands that his spouse is working as hard in the house as he is outside the house, and therefore, is entitled to half of his wealth and the same freedom and benefits that he wants for himself.

If you have put in time and effort in anything, you have not wasted your life.

THE END

M. Kukreja, M.D.

Made in United States
North Haven, CT
23 April 2022

18515393R00126